The Trauma Recovery Blueprint

The Trauma Recovery Blueprint:

A Practical Guide to Healing Your Nervous System, Rewiring Old Patterns, and Taking Back Your Life

Dr Don Russell, MA, Ed.D

Russell Healing Institute

This book is for educational purposes only and is not intended as a substitute for professional medical, psychological, or psychiatric care. The author is not responsible for how readers apply the information contained herein.

Printed in the United States of America

ISBN paperback 979-8-9940756-0-9

ISBN Hardcover 979-8-9940756-1-6

ISBN Audiobook 979-8-9940756-3-0

The author is a professional psychotherapist with over 30 years of clinical experience working in trauma recovery.

Dedication

This book is dedicated to those who learned to survive before they learned to feel safe.

To the people who adapted brilliantly to impossible situations, who kept going when their nervous systems were overwhelmed, and who are now gently learning that survival is no longer the only option.

May these pages help you remember that your responses were intelligent, your body was doing its best, and healing is not about fixing what is broken, but about restoring what was interrupted.

Acknowledgements

No book about healing is written alone. Healing happens in relationship, and so does learning and writing about healing. I want to acknowledge the many clients who have trusted me with their stories over the years. You have invited me in to your 'holy of holies', your sacred spaces of your heart. Although the examples in this book are carefully disguised and composite in nature, the wisdom reflected here belongs to those who allowed me to witness their courage, resilience, and persistence. You have taught me more about trauma, regulation, and healing than any textbook ever could.

I am deeply grateful to the clinicians, researchers, and teachers whose work informs these pages—particularly those in the fields of interpersonal neurobiology, attachment theory, somatic psychology, and trauma treatment. The contributions of thinkers such as Dan Siegel, Stephen Porges, Bessel van der Kolk, Peter Levine, Pat Ogden, Richard Schwartz, Francine Shapiro, and Philip Mansfield have shaped the way we understand trauma as a nervous system experience rather than a personal failure.

I also want to acknowledge my colleagues and mentors, whose thoughtful conversations, challenges, and shared curiosity have helped refine the ideas presented here. Healing happens in relationship, and so does good clinical thinking.

Finally, to my loved ones: Damaris, Cynthia, and Angelina—thank you for your patience, encouragement, and steady presence. Your support made the long hours of writing, revising, and reflecting not only possible, but meaningful.

Connect with Dr. Don

Youtube: @russellhealinginstituteltd

Instagram: www.instagram.com/drdonrussell/

Website: www.drdonrussell.com

A NOTE FROM DR. DON

Before you begin this book, I want to share something important about how it was written—and how it is meant to be used.

Writing this book, I was continually mindful of one central truth: trauma recovery cannot be rushed, forced, or solved through information alone.

Insight matters. Language matters. Understanding matters.

But healing happens through practice, pacing, and lived experience.

I have learned from helping people over 30 years, being invited into the sacred places of their heart that slower is faster.

That is why I created The Trauma Recovery Blueprint Workbook as a companion to this book.

The workbook was designed to help readers gently apply the concepts explored here—through reflection, nervous-system-aware exercises, and structured pauses that prioritize safety and choice. It is intentionally practical, flexible, and respectful of the fact that each person's healing process unfolds differently.

You do not need to complete every exercise, follow a strict order, or push yourself beyond what feels manageable. Healing works best when it is collaborative—not just between people, but within your own nervous system.

Whether you choose to continue with the workbook, professional support, or your own trusted practices, my hope is that this book has offered clarity, reassurance, and a deeper understanding of your own resilience.

Your nervous system learned to protect you.

It can also learn safety, connection, and integration—at its own pace.

— Dr. Don Russell

Tampa FL.

The Trauma Recovery Blueprint:

A Practical Guide to Healing Your Nervous System, Rewiring Old Patterns, and Taking Back Your Life

PART I Understanding Trauma & the Nervous System

Healing begins with understanding Before the nervous system can change, it helps to see clearly how trauma shapes perception, emotion, and reaction. Many responses that feel confusing or self-critical begin to make sense once we understand how the brain and body adapt to threat.

In this opening section, we explore the architecture of trauma: how the nervous system detects danger, how survival responses become patterned, and why past experiences can continue to influence the present long after the original events have ended.

Understanding does not resolve trauma by itself, but it creates something essential: compassion for the system that has been trying to protect you all along.

Chapter 1 - When The Body Remembers

> *"The heart has its reasons of which reason knows nothing".* - Blaise Pascal - French philosopher and theologian

There is often a quiet moment when awareness begins.

It is not dramatic or cinematic. It does not arrive with a clear label that says trauma. More often, it appears as a subtle dissonance — standing at the kitchen sink with an unexplained tightness in your chest, reacting strongly to something small, or lying awake at night with an ache you cannot quite name.

You might tell yourself, This shouldn't still bother me. You might remind yourself that it happened years ago, or that other people had it worse. And yet your body continues to respond as if something is happening now.

This is where many people begin: confused by the gap between what they know intellectually and what they feel physiologically.

Trauma Is Not Just an Event

When we hear the word trauma, we often imagine catastrophic events — war, assault, disaster. And yes, those experiences can absolutely overwhelm the nervous system. But trauma is not defined solely by the size of an event. It is defined by its impact.

Trauma occurs when an experience overwhelms your capacity to cope at the time it happens. It is less about objective severity and more about the internal experience of helplessness, fear, isolation, or loss of control. Two people can walk through the same situation and emerge differently. One nervous system integrates the experience; the other organizes around it.

This difference is not a measure of strength or weakness. It is a reflection of biology, history, context, and relational support. When an experience exceeds what your system can process, it is stored differently.

The nervous system is constantly scanning for cues of safety or threat. Long before conscious thought forms, your body is evaluating tone of voice, facial expression, movement, distance, silence. This happens automatically and continuously.

When something overwhelming occurs, the nervous system shifts into survival mode. If the experience cannot be processed and integrated, it becomes stored not primarily as narrative memory, but as sensation, emotion, and implicit expectation.

This is why you might find your heart racing without knowing why. Why you shut down during a conversation that vaguely resembles something from long ago. Why certain environments feel unsafe even when logic tells you they are not. Why shame, anger, or fear can surge seemingly out of nowhere.

Your body is not malfunctioning. It is remembering. When the nervous system detects threat, it activates survival responses automatically—fight, flight, freeze, submit, attach. These are not choices. They are reflexive patterns designed to protect life.

If fighting worked, your system learned to mobilize quickly.

If escaping worked, it learned to withdraw.

If freezing minimized harm, stillness became protective.

If compliance kept you safer, appeasement became adaptive.

Over time, these responses can crystallize into relational and emotional patterns. What once protected you may now interfere with intimacy, work, or self-trust. But every pattern began as an intelligent attempt at survival.

When we understand this, shame begins to soften. Instead of asking, What's wrong with me? we begin to ask, What did my system learn?

Why Insight Alone Does Not Resolve Trauma

Many thoughtful, reflective people understand their history quite well. They can describe what happened. They can analyze family dynamics. They may have read extensively about trauma and attachment. And yet, despite insight, their body continues to react.

This is because trauma is not stored primarily in language. It is stored in physiology.

You cannot reason your way out of a nervous system response any more than you can think your way out of a reflex. If your hand touches a hot stove, it withdraws before your mind explains what happened. In much the same way, trauma responses are fast, automatic, and embodied.

Healing requires working with the nervous system, not arguing against it.

Neuroscientist Dan Siegel introduced the concept of the window of tolerance — the zone in which the nervous system can think, feel, and respond effectively. Within this window, we can tolerate emotional intensity without becoming overwhelmed. We can stay connected to ourselves and others. We can reflect rather than react. When we move outside this window, two broad patterns emerge.

In hyperarousal, the system mobilizes. Anxiety rises, anger flares, thoughts race, and the body feels charged. In hypoarousal, the system conserves. We may feel numb, foggy, disconnected, or shut down.

Trauma narrows this window. Situations that others navigate with relative ease may push a trauma-impacted nervous system into activation or collapse.

Understanding this reframes the question entirely. Rather than asking, Why am I overreacting?

we begin to ask, Where is my nervous system right now?

That question opens the door to compassion and skill-building rather than self-criticism.

The nervous system is not fixed. Neuroplasticity — the brain's capacity to change through experience — means that patterns formed in survival can reorganize toward safety.

This does not occur through willpower alone. It unfolds through regulation, connection, awareness, and repeated experiences of safety. It happens as we learn to notice early signs of activation. As we practice returning to the present moment. As we experience relationships that feel steady and predictable. As we allow the body to complete responses that were once interrupted.

Healing is not about erasing the past. It is about teaching the nervous system that the present is different.

If trauma lives in the nervous system, then healing must reach the nervous system as well. It cannot be forced through insight alone, nor rushed simply because we are tired of carrying it.

The body organized itself around protection for a reason. What we often label as "overreacting" is usually the nervous system doing exactly what it was trained to do. But here is the hopeful truth: the same nervous system that learned survival can learn safety.

Healing is not random. There is a developmental arc to it — a movement from stabilization to regulation, from isolation to connection, from survival to integration. When we begin to understand how the nervous system works, we begin to see our symptoms differently. They are not evidence of weakness. They are evidence of adaptation. And adaptation can evolve.

In the next chapter, we will begin exploring the biological architecture beneath your reactions — the systems that shape your emotions, your relationships, and your sense of safety. As we build that foundation, you may begin to recognize something deeply important: Your nervous system has always been trying to protect you. Now, it can begin to help you live.

Chapter 2 - The Architecture of Protection

The paradox of trauma is that it has both the power to destroy and the power to transform and resurrect. - Peter Levine

If your nervous system learned to protect you, then the next question is unavoidable: How did it learn?

In the previous chapter, we explored the possibility that your reactions are not signs of weakness, immaturity, or dysfunction. They are signs of adaptation. Your body did what it had to do to survive what you lived through. But survival is not random. It is patterned. It follows design.

To understand healing, we must first understand the architecture that made adaptation possible.

Your nervous system is not merely a network of nerves. It is an exquisitely tuned detection system —

constantly asking, beneath conscious thought: 'Am I safe? This question is not philosophical. It is biological'.

Long before you form a belief about danger, your body has already scanned tone of voice, posture, proximity, speed of movement, facial expression, silence, unpredictability. It does this automatically. You do not choose it. You inherit it.

Neuroscientist Stephen Porges calls this process neuroception — the nervous system's ability to detect safety or threat without conscious reasoning. Neuroception does not wait for evidence. It responds to cues.

If cues signal safety, your body remains open and engaged. If cues signal threat, your body shifts into protection.

You may not notice the shift at first. It can be subtle: a tightening in the chest, a narrowing of focus, a slight rise in heart rate. But beneath that subtle change is an ancient cascade of physiology preparing you to survive.

The Three Survival Pathways

For simplicity, we can understand the nervous system as operating within three primary survival pathways.

When you feel grounded, curious, connected, and able to think clearly, your system is in what we call the social engagement state. Your breathing is steady. Your heart rhythm is regulated. Your facial muscles are flexible enough to express emotion and receive it from others. In this state, you can reflect, repair conflict, solve problems, and experience intimacy.

When your system detects threat, it mobilizes. This is the sympathetic response — often described as fight or flight. Your heart rate accelerates. Blood flows toward large muscles. Attention sharpens. You may feel anxiety, urgency, anger, or defensive energy. This state is not pathology. It is readiness.

If threat feels overwhelming or inescapable, the system may shift into immobilization — sometimes described as freeze or collapse. Energy drops. Muscles may feel heavy. Thinking slows. Emotional numbness or dissociation can emerge. This state is not weakness. It is conservation — the body's final line of defense when mobilization is not enough.

These pathways are adaptive. Each one evolved to preserve life. The difficulty arises when the system remains in protection long after the original threat has passed.

How Experience Becomes Pattern

The nervous system learns through repetition. If a child grows up in an unpredictable environment — where emotional outbursts or withdrawal are common — the system becomes vigilant. It scans constantly. Over time, hyperarousal feels normal. Decades later, that adult may find their heart racing during mild conflict. The reaction feels disproportionate, but the nervous system is responding to similarity, not logic.

If a child repeatedly experiences overwhelm without rescue, immobilization may become familiar. As an adult, shutting down during stress may occur automatically. The body is not choosing defeat. It is choosing survival.

The nervous system does not store trauma as narrative memory alone. It stores it as activation pattern.

This is why someone can say, "I know this is different now," and still feel their body react as though it isn't.

Your biology moves faster than your reasoning. Perhaps one of the most powerful truths about the nervous system is that it shapes not only sensation, but interpretation.

When you are regulated, your thinking expands. You assume complexity. You tolerate ambiguity. You consider alternatives.

When you are mobilized, your thoughts narrow. You scan for threat. You replay conversations. You prepare for the worst.

When you are immobilized, hope can dim. Effort feels exhausting. The world appears smaller and less promising.

The body's state influences the mind's story. This is why trauma recovery cannot rely on insight alone. You cannot think your way into safety if your body remains in defense. Regulation precedes clarity.

Borrowed Safety

The hopeful counterpoint to all of this is relational. From infancy onward, human nervous systems regulate together. A calm caregiver steadies a distressed child. Eye contact slows breathing. Gentle tone reduces heart rate. This process is not metaphorical. It is measurable.

As adults, we continue to regulate in relationship. You can feel it when you enter a tense room. You can feel it when someone grounded sits across from you. Your body responds before your thoughts catch up.

Trauma often disrupts this co-regulation. It teaches the system that closeness may not equal safety. But healing frequently restores it. A steady presence — therapist, partner, friend — becomes a new template. Over time, your nervous system internalizes that template and expands its capacity.

Connection is not optional in recovery. It is biological.

If the nervous system learned protection through experience, then it can learn safety the same way — through new experience. This is where hope enters.

The system is plastic. It changes in response to repeated, embodied experience. Every time you return to calm after activation, you strengthen a pathway. Every time you remain present during mild stress, you expand your window of tolerance. Every time you experience safe connection, you widen your capacity for intimacy.

Healing is not the erasure of protection. It is the integration of it. Your nervous system is not broken. It is patterned. And patterns can change.

In the next chapter, we will begin mapping that change more explicitly. If the nervous system organizes around protection, how do we guide it toward integration? What stages does recovery naturally follow? And how do we move from surviving to becoming whole?

We now understand the architecture. Next, we begin working with the blueprint.

Chapter 3 - The RNSI Model™

A Developmental Framework for Trauma Recovery

If trauma reorganizes the nervous system, then healing must reorganize it as well.

Over three decades of clinical work — informed by attachment science, interpersonal neurobiology, somatic psychology, and trauma research — I began to notice something remarkably consistent beneath the apparent complexity of trauma recovery.

While every person's story is unique, the nervous system tends to heal through recognizable developmental processes.

Recovery is not random. It is organized. Not mechanically organized, but biologically organized.

Again and again, I observed that durable healing followed a predictable sequence. When individuals attempted advanced trauma work before sufficient stabilization, they often became overwhelmed. When emotional regulation developed without relational repair, deeper intimacy remained difficult. When insight occurred without nervous system integration, old survival patterns quickly resurfaced under stress.

The nervous system appeared to require certain capacities before it could safely develop the next.

From these observations emerged what I now call the **Relational Nervous System Integration Model™** — a developmental framework describing how trauma recovery unfolds through progressive stages of nervous system reorganization.

This model rests on two foundational principles:

1. Trauma is fundamentally a nervous system phenomenon.

2. Healing occurs through regulated relational experience — including the relationship we develop with our own body, emotions, and internal states.

Trauma is not simply stored as memory. It is stored as altered physiology.

The body learns vigilance. Constriction. Dissociation. Hyperactivation. Collapse.

Healing therefore requires more than insight alone. It requires new lived experiences capable of reshaping the nervous system itself.

The Relational Nervous System Integration Model™ describes five interconnected stages of recovery:

1. Stabilization — establishing physiological safety
2. Regulation — developing flexible nervous system control
3. Attachment Repair — restoring relational security
4. Integration — metabolizing traumatic memory
5. Embodied Expansion — reorganizing life around growth rather than survival

These stages are not rigid compartments. Healing is rarely linear. People often move back and forth between stages, revisiting earlier capacities at deeper levels over time.

But while recovery is nonlinear, it is not arbitrary. Sequence matters.

Each stage creates the conditions necessary for the next. Attempting later-stage work without earlier-stage capacity frequently produces destabilization rather than transformation.

You cannot sustainably process overwhelming traumatic material without sufficient regulation. You cannot fully trust intimacy while the nervous system still anticipates danger in connection. And you cannot build an expansive life while large portions of your physiology remain organized around survival.

This model is therefore not merely descriptive. It is developmental.

Each stage solves a specific nervous system problem created by trauma:

Stabilization addresses overwhelming activation.

Regulation addresses autonomic rigidity.

Attachment repair addresses relational threat expectancy.

Integration addresses unresolved implicit memory.

Embodied expansion restores adaptive growth, creativity, intimacy, and purpose.

Together, these stages describe the gradual movement from survival organization toward integrated coherence.

Let us examine each stage more closely.

Stage One: Stabilization

Before trauma can be processed, the nervous system must experience sufficient safety.

In early recovery, many individuals understandably want to "get to the root" of their trauma as quickly as possible. Yet if the system remains outside its window of tolerance — oscillating between hyperarousal and shutdown — direct trauma processing can unintentionally reinforce dysregulation.

Stabilization is therefore not avoidance. It is neurobiological preparation.

In this stage, the primary clinical task is increasing the nervous system's capacity to remain within tolerable activation. This includes grounding practices, orienting exercises, breath regulation, environmental predictability, and strengthening present-time awareness. It also involves identifying triggers and learning to recognize early signs of escalation before overwhelm occurs.

The goal is not perpetual calm. That is not realistic.

The goal is safety, predictability, and sufficient physiological containment.

Without stabilization, deeper work overwhelms the system. With stabilization, the nervous system gradually learns that activation does not necessarily equal annihilation.

That realization becomes the platform for everything that follows.

Stage Two: Regulation

If stabilization establishes safety, regulation develops flexibility.

Regulation is the growing ability to notice shifts in internal state and influence them intentionally. It transforms automatic reactivity into increasing responsiveness.

Earlier we explored how the autonomic nervous system moves among states of social engagement, mobilization, and immobilization. In this stage, individuals begin learning to recognize these shifts in real time. They discover how breath, posture, movement, sensory input, attention, and relational contact influence autonomic activation.

This is not emotional suppression. It is skilled modulation of arousal.

As regulation strengthens, the nervous system becomes less afraid of its own activation. Emotional intensity may still arise, but it no longer feels catastrophic or uncontrollable. Individuals develop increased affect tolerance — the capacity to remain present with emotional experience without fragmenting, dissociating, or becoming overwhelmed.

Regulation creates the internal flexibility required for deeper relational healing.

Stage Three: Attachment Repair

Many traumatic wounds are relational in origin. They formed in environments where safety, attunement, protection, or emotional consistency were unreliable, overwhelming, or absent.

Because the nervous system develops through co-regulation, early attachment experiences shape long-term expectations of connection. When caregiving relationships are frightening, chaotic, rejecting, or emotionally unavailable, the nervous system adapts accordingly.

The body learns that closeness may not be safe.

Attachment repair involves corrective relational experience.

This may occur within therapy through consistent attunement, emotional repair, and secure relational presence. It may develop within healthy friendships, partnerships, communities, or spiritual relationships. It may also emerge internally as individuals learn to respond to their own distress with compassion rather than criticism.

Repeated experiences of safe connection gradually recalibrate the nervous system's expectations.

The body begins learning that closeness does not necessarily signal danger. Conflict no longer automatically predicts abandonment. Needs become more tolerable to experience and express.

Earned secure attachment is not merely a psychological concept. It is a physiological reorganization of relational expectation.

With sufficient relational safety established, the nervous system can begin approaching traumatic material without becoming overwhelmed.

Stage Four: Integration

Integration is the structured reprocessing of traumatic memory. Trauma fragments experience. Sensory impressions, emotional states, beliefs, and defensive responses become stored in implicit memory networks disconnected from present context. The nervous system reacts as though the past is still occurring.

Integration reconnects memory with time.

Evidence-based approaches such as EMDR, Sensorimotor Psychotherapy, Flash Technique, somatic therapies, and other experiential modalities help facilitate this reconnection. Through carefully regulated activation, previously overwhelming material becomes metabolized rather than endlessly re-enacted.

The objective is not erasure. It is transformation.

When integration occurs, traumatic memories remain autobiographical rather than physiological. The nervous system no longer mobilizes reflexively in response to reminders of the past. The body recognizes that the danger is over.

This marks a profound shift from survival-based organization toward adaptive coherence.

Stage Five: Embodied Expansion

Healing is not complete when symptoms diminish. Healing culminates in expansion.

As regulation stabilizes and trauma integrates, energy previously devoted to protection becomes available for creativity, intimacy, leadership, exploration, spirituality, contribution, and purpose. The nervous system reorganizes around growth rather than threat detection.

Individuals often describe this stage not simply as "feeling better," but as feeling more fully alive — more fully themselves.

Embodied expansion reflects restored flexibility, emotional range, relational depth, spontaneity, and vitality. It includes the capacity to experience joy without bracing for catastrophe, to pursue goals without chronic vigilance, and to remain connected during stress rather than automatically collapsing into survival defenses.

This stage does not represent perfection. It represents integration.

The nervous system no longer spends most of its energy trying to survive the past. It becomes increasingly free to inhabit the present.

Why the Sequence Matters

Clinical experience consistently demonstrates that bypassing developmental stages compromises recovery. Trauma processing without stabilization destabilizes.

Regulation without relational repair limits depth.

Attachment work without integration leaves implicit survival memory largely intact. Trauma recovery is developmental because the nervous system itself develops developmentally.

It must first experience safety. Then flexibility. Then relational trust.

Only then can it safely reorganize traumatic memory and expand into fuller adaptive functioning.

The Relational Nervous System Integration Model™ provides a roadmap grounded in neurobiology, attachment science, somatic psychology, and decades of clinical observation. It offers a framework for understanding not only what healing involves, but why recovery unfolds in the sequence that it does.

In the chapters ahead, we will move through these stages deliberately.

We will begin by strengthening stabilization and regulation capacity, then examine attachment patterns, memory integration, and eventually the broader process of embodied coherence and expansion.

If you developed trauma survival responses, that does not mean you are defective.

Your nervous system adapted intelligently to what it experienced. And with the right sequence of relational and physiological experience, it can reorganize toward health.

You now have a map.

Chapter 4 - Stage One: Stabilization

"We have learned that trauma is not just an event that took place sometime in the past; it is also the imprint left by that experience on mind, brain, and body." — Bessel van der Kolk

If Chapter 3 introduced the architecture of the Relational Nervous System Integration Model™, this chapter begins the first developmental task of recovery: establishing stabilization.

Within this model, stabilization is not merely symptom management.

It is the physiological foundation upon which all subsequent healing depends.

Before the nervous system can safely revisit traumatic memory, it must first develop sufficient capacity for regulation, orientation, and present-time safety. Without that foundation, trauma work often becomes overwhelming rather than transformative.

This is why nearly every major phase-oriented trauma model begins here.

Judith Herman identified safety and stabilization as the first stage of trauma recovery decades ago. Contemporary neuroscience has only deepened our understanding of why this sequence matters so profoundly. When the nervous system becomes dysregulated, higher-order cortical functioning becomes compromised. The brain's capacity for reflection, integration, reasoning, and emotional modulation diminishes significantly.

In simple terms: a dysregulated brain cannot process trauma safely.

This principle is foundational to the Relational Nervous System Integration Model™. Stage One is therefore not about "fixing" emotions or eliminating distress. It is about helping the nervous system become sufficiently safe, flexible, and regulated to tolerate deeper healing work without fragmentation or overwhelm.

Stabilization teaches the body something profoundly important: activation is survivable.

That lesson changes everything.

The Neurobiology of Stabilization

Trauma fundamentally alters the nervous system's relationship to safety.

After overwhelming experiences, the body often begins operating as though danger remains ongoing. The autonomic nervous system becomes biased toward protection rather than flexibility. Some individuals become chronically hyperactivated — anxious, vigilant, restless, emotionally flooded. Others move toward shutdown — numbness, exhaustion, dissociation, emotional flattening, cognitive fog.

Many alternate between both. These are not character flaws. They are adaptive survival responses. The nervous system is attempting to protect the organism using the strategies available to it.

One of the most useful frameworks for understanding this process comes from Dan Siegel and his concept of the *window of tolerance*. Within this optimal zone of arousal, the nervous system remains sufficiently regulated for integrated functioning. Emotional activation can occur without overwhelming the individual's ability to think, reflect, remain present, and stay connected.

Outside that window, integration begins to collapse.

Hyperarousal reflects excessive sympathetic activation:

- racing heart
- shallow breathing
- intrusive thoughts
- emotional flooding
- impulsive reactions
- hypervigilance

Hypoarousal reflects immobilization and dorsal vagal shutdown:

- numbness
- dissociation
- exhaustion
- cognitive fog
- emotional flattening
- disconnection

Neither state is pathological in itself. Both are evolutionarily conserved survival responses.

The problem is not that the nervous system learned these strategies. The problem is that it no longer knows when to stop using them.

Stage One stabilization work gradually increases autonomic flexibility. Through repeated experiences of grounding, orientation, breath regulation, sensory awareness, movement, and safe relational contact, the nervous system begins learning how to return to baseline more efficiently after activation.

This is not abstract theory. It is measurable physiology.

Research involving heart rate variability, affect regulation, autonomic flexibility, and polyvagal functioning increasingly points toward the same conclusion: flexibility is resilience.

A healthy nervous system is not one that never becomes activated. It is one that can move into activation and reliably return from it.

Why We Do Not Begin With Trauma Processing

Many people understandably want to “go directly to the wound.” They want insight. Explanation. Emotional release. Resolution.

But premature trauma processing often overwhelms a nervous system that lacks sufficient regulatory capacity.

Research on affect tolerance and exposure-based therapies consistently demonstrates that activation beyond manageable limits can reinforce fear circuitry rather than resolve it. When traumatic memory becomes too overwhelming, the nervous system stops integrating and shifts back into survival mode.

This is why stabilization must come first. Before deep trauma processing becomes therapeutic, the nervous system must first learn several critical experiences:

Activation can be survived

Emotion can be tolerated

Regulation is accessible

Safety can be restored

The body can return from distress

Only then does memory processing become reorganizing rather than retraumatizing. Stabilization is therefore not avoidance. It is preparation.

Within the Relational Nervous System Integration Model™, Stage One establishes the physiological container capable of eventually holding deeper emotional and relational work.

Without that container, the nervous system fragments.

With it, healing becomes possible

A Clinical Illustration: Mandy

Mandy was a nineteen-year-old college student who came to see me for severe test anxiety.

On the surface, her presenting problem did not initially appear trauma-related. She described "freezing" during exams. Her mind would go blank. Her hands trembled. Her stomach tightened. Sometimes she became so overwhelmed she could barely read the questions in front of her.

Neurobiologically, however, her nervous system was displaying a classic survival response.

Her body was not interpreting the exam as an academic challenge. It was interpreting it as threat.

Research on performance anxiety demonstrates that excessive cortisol and adrenaline impair working memory and executive functioning. As sympathetic activation rises beyond tolerable levels, the prefrontal cortex becomes less efficient. Reasoning, recall, concentration, and cognitive flexibility begin to deteriorate.

In Mandy's case, her body was not malfunctioning. It was protecting her.

As we explored her history, we discovered repeated experiences of criticism, humiliation, and emotional invalidation surrounding academic performance during childhood. Over time, her nervous system had encoded evaluation itself as danger.

Importantly, Stage One work did not begin by deeply processing those childhood memories. It began with physiology.

We practiced paced breathing. Sensory orientation. Muscle relaxation. Grounding. Present-time awareness. We taught her nervous system how to remain within tolerable activation during evaluative situations.

Gradually, something began to shift.

Her body started associating exams with manageable activation rather than catastrophe. Her autonomic nervous system became more flexible. Her window of tolerance widened.

Stabilization changed the pattern because stabilization changed the physiology beneath the pattern.

Mandy's story illustrates an essential truth of Stage One: anxiety is rarely random.

The nervous system learns associations through experience, and many symptoms that appear irrational make profound neurobiological sense once we understand the survival adaptations beneath them.

Stabilization as the Beginning of Reorganization

Stage One is often misunderstood as "basic coping skills." In reality, stabilization initiates the earliest phases of nervous system reorganization.

Every moment of successful grounding slightly weakens helplessness. Every experience of returning from activation strengthens predictability. Every regulated breath teaches the body that survival no longer requires constant alarm.

These moments may appear small externally. Neurobiologically, they are profound.

The nervous system slowly begins shifting from chronic threat anticipation toward increasing safety and flexibility. This is the beginning of recovery.

But stabilization involves more than managing anxiety and activation. Sometimes the nervous system's protective strategies become more complex. When overwhelming experience exceeds the brain's capacity to integrate, the mind may compartmentalize awareness itself.

To understand those deeper protective adaptations, we must now explore dissociation — the brain's remarkable ability to divide conscious experience in order to survive.

Stage One continues by examining what happens when activation becomes too overwhelming for the nervous system to contain.

Chapter 5 - Surfing the Waves of Activation

"You can't stop the waves, but you can learn to surf."

— Jon Kabat-Zinn

In the previous chapter, we began exploring Stage One of the Relational Nervous System Integration Model™: stabilization.

We examined why the nervous system must first develop sufficient safety and flexibility before deeper trauma processing can occur. Stabilization is not simply about "calming down." It is about increasing the body's capacity to remain present during activation without becoming overwhelmed, shutting down, or fragmenting.

This chapter deepens that work by examining one of the most important capacities developed during

Stage One: the ability to stay present while waves of activation move through the body.

Trauma recovery requires more than understanding emotions intellectually. It requires learning how to experience activation physiologically without being consumed by it.

That process begins by recognizing that anxiety is not random. It is patterned survival energy.

Mandy and the Physiology of Threat

Mandy, whom we met briefly in the previous chapter, was nineteen years old when she first came to see me.

She was intelligent, articulate, and academically capable. Yet she described what she called "crippling test anxiety." The night before exams she could not sleep. Her heart raced. Her thoughts spiraled uncontrollably. During the exam itself, her mind often went blank. At times she felt as though she disappeared internally while sitting at her desk.

"I know the material," she insisted. "But when I sit down at that desk, I shut down."

From the outside, this appeared to be anxiety. From a nervous system perspective, it was something more precise: her body was interpreting evaluation as threat.

Modern neuroscience has demonstrated that under perceived danger, the sympathetic branch of the autonomic nervous system mobilizes the body for survival. Cortisol and adrenaline increase. Heart rate accelerates. Muscles tighten. Blood flow shifts away from higher cortical regions toward systems involved in immediate protection and rapid response.

In genuine danger, this response is adaptive. In a classroom, it becomes disruptive.

Research on performance anxiety consistently demonstrates that excessive stress activation impairs working memory and executive functioning. As activation rises beyond tolerable limits, the prefrontal cortex becomes less efficient. Reasoning, concentration, recall, and cognitive flexibility all begin to deteriorate.

Under excessive activation, we lose access to the very neural systems required for complex thinking.

Mandy's blank mind was therefore not evidence of weakness or incompetence. It was evidence of nervous system overactivation.

How the Nervous System Learns Threat

As we explored Mandy's history, a pattern gradually emerged. Throughout childhood, she had repeatedly experienced criticism, humiliation, and emotional pressure surrounding academic performance. Mistakes were not treated as developmental experiences. They were treated as failures of worth. Shame frequently followed imperfection.

Over time, her nervous system learned several powerful associations:

- Evaluation equals danger
- Mistakes equal humiliation
- Visibility equals threat
- Performance determines safety

Importantly, these associations no longer existed merely as thoughts. They had become physiological predictions.

By adulthood, her body reacted automatically before conscious reasoning even entered the process. The exam desk itself had become a trigger for sympathetic activation.

This illustrates one of the central principles of Stage One stabilization: the nervous system learns through repetition. Trauma is not simply remembered cognitively. It is anticipated physiologically.

The body begins preparing for danger before the conscious mind fully understands why.

Stabilization Before Insight

It would have been tempting to immediately begin processing Mandy's childhood experiences. But Stage One work requires patience and sequence.

Before deeper memory integration can occur, the nervous system must first learn that activation is tolerable, survivable, and modifiable. Otherwise, therapeutic work risks overwhelming the system rather than reorganizing it.

So we began not with memory, but with physiology.

Before studying, Mandy practiced paced diaphragmatic breathing. During mock testing scenarios, she learned to orient visually to the room, feel her feet against the floor, lengthen her exhale, and monitor early signs of activation in her body.

She learned to notice:

tightening in her jaw

shallow breathing

narrowing attention

increased muscular tension

accelerated thoughts

These were not merely "relaxation techniques." They were nervous system retraining.

Gradually, something important began to shift.

For the first time, Mandy discovered that she could influence her internal state rather than simply be overtaken by it. The activation no longer felt entirely uncontrollable. She could remain present while the wave moved through her body.

The nervous system slowly began updating its predictions. An exam no longer automatically triggered catastrophic threat. It triggered manageable activation.

This is one of the central developmental tasks of stabilization: helping the nervous system experience activation without equating it with annihilation.

The Physiology of Surfing

Anxiety often feels like an enemy that must be eliminated. But from a neurobiological perspective, anxiety is fundamentally mobilization energy.

It is activation preparing the organism for action.

The goal of stabilization is therefore not suppression. It is modulation.

Imagine a wave forming offshore. If the wave builds unchecked, it crashes violently. But if you understand its rhythm, movement, and timing, you can learn to ride it rather than be consumed by it.

Stage One stabilization teaches precisely this capacity.

It teaches individuals how to surf activation.

Trauma researchers often refer to this as increasing affect tolerance — the ability to remain present with emotional intensity without becoming overwhelmed, dissociated, or emotionally flooded.

Affect tolerance is not developed through force or willpower.

It develops through repeated experiences of:

safe activation

successful regulation

return to baseline

physiological recovery

Each time Mandy entered an exam and successfully regulated her breathing, oriented to the room, and remained present through rising activation, her nervous system learned something new:

Activation can rise.

Activation can fall.

I can remain present.

I do not disappear.

I can return.

Over time, the body gradually learned what the mind already knew: the exam was not life-threatening.

This is how stabilization begins reshaping survival patterns.

Not through intellectual insight alone, but through repeated corrective physiological experience.

When Activation Becomes Too Much

Mandy's pattern reflected relatively straightforward sympathetic overactivation. But not all nervous system adaptations are so linear.

Sometimes activation exceeds the system's capacity to mobilize effectively. When fight or flight no longer appears possible, the nervous system may shift into an entirely different survival strategy: disconnection.

This can appear as:

numbness

detachment

cognitive fog

emotional absence

depersonalization

fragmentation of experience

From the outside, these states may appear confusing or irrational.

Neurobiologically, however, they are profoundly intelligent survival adaptations. The nervous system disconnects in order to reduce overwhelming distress.

Stage One stabilization therefore involves more than calming hyperactivation. It also involves strengthening the nervous system's ability to remain present during emotionally intense experience without disappearing into fragmentation or shutdown.

To understand these deeper protective adaptations, we must now explore dissociation — the brain's remarkable ability to divide conscious experience in order to survive overwhelming conditions.

Stabilization is not only about calming the waves. It is also about learning not to disappear beneath them.

Chapter 6 - When the Mind Divides

"Two entirely distinct states of consciousness were present which alternated very frequently and without warning and which became more and more differentiated in the course of the illness."

— Sigmund Freud and Josef Breuer, Studies in Hysteria

In the previous chapters, we explored how the nervous system mobilizes under threat.

We examined anxiety, sympathetic activation, and the body's tendency to organize itself around protection when danger is anticipated. We also explored how Stage One stabilization within the Relational Nervous System Integration Model™ gradually increases the nervous system's capacity to remain present during activation rather than becoming overwhelmed by it.

But mobilization is not always possible.

There are situations — especially in early life — where fight or flight are unavailable options.

A child cannot escape a parent. A dependent person cannot safely confront a caregiver. A restrained body cannot flee.

When action becomes impossible, the nervous system deploys another survival strategy. It divides. Dissociation is not a defect of character. It is an adaptive protective response.

When activation becomes overwhelming and escape is blocked, consciousness itself may fragment in order to preserve psychological survival. The mind separates aspects of experience that would otherwise feel intolerable.

To understand dissociation clearly, we must shift from thinking about trauma merely as something that happened to a person and begin understanding trauma as something the nervous system did in order to survive overwhelming conditions.

This distinction matters profoundly.

Because what the nervous system learned adaptively can eventually be reorganized safely.

The Neurobiology of Leaving

When threat escalates beyond what sympathetic mobilization can effectively manage, the autonomic nervous system may shift into a state of dorsal vagal dominance — a physiological state characterized by immobilization, numbing, shutdown, and disconnection.

Heart rate may slow. Blood pressure may drop. The body becomes still.

The external world can begin feeling distant, muted, dreamlike, or unreal. This is not collapse as failure. It is collapse as protection.

From an evolutionary perspective, dissociation reduces conscious exposure to overwhelming pain, terror, helplessness, or entrapment. The nervous system prioritizes survival over full integration of experience.

Neuroimaging studies increasingly demonstrate that during dissociative states, activity in regions associated with emotional processing, autobiographical memory, bodily awareness, and integration becomes significantly altered. Memory encoding itself becomes fragmented. Rather than being stored as coherent narrative, traumatic experience is often encoded as:

sensory fragments

bodily sensations

emotional flashes

disconnected images

implicit survival states

This helps explain why trauma survivors frequently say things such as:

"I know it happened, but it doesn't feel real."

"Parts of it are missing."

"It feels far away and overwhelming at the same time."

The mind protected itself by reducing integration. Fragmentation was not weakness. It was survival intelligence.

Fragmentation as Adaptation

Let me offer a clinical example.

James came to therapy describing episodes of "losing time" during conflict with his partner. As tension escalated, he would suddenly feel detached from himself, as though watching the interaction from outside his body. His partner's voice sounded muffled and distant, almost underwater. At times he struggled to remember portions of the conversation afterward.

Importantly, James was not consciously choosing this response. His body was.

As we explored his history, we uncovered repeated experiences of unpredictable anger and emotional volatility during childhood. As a young boy, he had learned something critical: when danger escalated, emotional disappearance reduced risk.

His nervous system encoded a survival strategy:

stay small

stay quiet

disconnect internally

disappear psychologically

Years later, during relational conflict, those same neural circuits activated automatically. His dissociation was not immaturity. It was preserved survival physiology.

This is one of the most important reframes within trauma treatment many symptoms that appear irrational make profound neurobiological sense once we understand the survival adaptations beneath them.

Stabilization and the Expansion of Presence

Within Stage One of the Relational Nervous System Integration Model™, the goal is not to forcibly eliminate dissociation immediately.

Attempting to abruptly "break through" dissociation can actually destabilize the nervous system further if sufficient regulation capacity has not yet developed.

Instead, stabilization work focuses first on increasing awareness and strengthening presence gradually.

With James, we began by helping him recognize the earliest signals that dissociation was beginning to emerge:

narrowing vision

fading sound

heaviness in the body

slowed cognition

emotional distance

a sense of drifting away internally

These cues represented the nervous system attempting to move toward protection.

As James learned to notice these transitions earlier, something important began to change.

Instead of disappearing completely, he could remain partially present. Over time, partial presence became fuller presence.

This is often how stabilization unfolds. Not dramatically. Incrementally.

Seconds of presence become minutes. Small moments of grounding become increasing continuity of awareness. The nervous system gradually learns that activation can be tolerated without complete fragmentation.

Within Stage One, stabilization is therefore not simply about calming anxiety.

It is about strengthening the nervous system's capacity to remain connected to experience without needing to disappear from it.

Dissociation Exists on a Spectrum

Many people associate dissociation only with severe trauma or extreme psychological disorders.

In reality, dissociative responses exist on a continuum.

Milder forms may include:

daydreaming during stress

going blank during confrontation

emotional numbing

detachment during medical procedures

feeling absent during conflict

"checking out" under pressure

At the more severe end, dissociation may involve:

depersonalization

derealization

memory gaps

identity fragmentation

distinct self-states

But across this spectrum, the underlying purpose remains remarkably consistent: to reduce unbearable internal experience.

The nervous system prioritizes survival over coherence.

Seen through this lens, dissociation becomes far less mysterious. The mind divided because full contact with overwhelming experience exceeded the system's capacity to tolerate it safely.

Why Stabilization Must Precede Integration

This is precisely why stabilization must precede deeper trauma processing.

Premature exposure to overwhelming traumatic material can amplify fragmentation in a nervous system that lacks sufficient regulatory capacity. Research across phase-oriented trauma treatment models consistently demonstrates that trauma processing becomes destabilizing when the nervous system cannot remain sufficiently present during activation.

The Relational Nervous System Integration Model™ follows this same developmental logic.

Before deeper integration can occur, the nervous system must first develop:

regulation capacity

affect tolerance

present-time orientation

bodily awareness

internal predictability

sufficient relational safety

Only then can traumatic material be approached without overwhelming the system.

Stabilization is therefore not avoidance of trauma work. It is preparation for trauma work.

And there is something profoundly hopeful embedded within dissociation itself.

The fact that the mind could divide means that parts of the self were preserved.

Trauma did not destroy the self. It protected it.

From Protection Toward Connection

In the next phase of healing, we begin widening outward beyond internal stabilization alone.

Because while dissociation protects against danger, healing ultimately requires reconnection. Connection with the body. Connection with emotion. Connection with memory. Connection with other people.

If Stage One has focused primarily on establishing safety within the self, the next developmental movement within the Relational Nervous System Integration Model™ begins exploring how relationships themselves shape nervous system regulation.

In the chapters ahead, we will examine attachment, co-regulation, relational safety, and the ways human connection reorganizes the nervous system over time.

The mind divided to survive. It reconnects to heal.

PART II - Rebuilding Regulation & Internal Stability

Once we understand how trauma shapes the nervous system, the next step is learning how to restore balance.

Trauma narrows the range of emotional and physiological states that feel manageable. The nervous system may move quickly into anxiety, shutdown, or overwhelm, leaving little room for flexibility.

This section focuses on rebuilding that flexibility.

Through awareness, regulation practices, and a deeper understanding of how the body organizes experience, the nervous system begins to rediscover its natural capacity to return to safety. These skills form thc foundation for all deeper healing work.

Before trauma can be fully processed, the body must first learn that it can remain present.

Chapter 7 - Stage Two: Relational Regulation

How Attachment Shapes the Nervous System

"Children are like wet cement. Whatever falls on them makes an impression."

— Haim Ginott

In Stage One of the Relational Nervous System Integration Model™, we focused on stabilization within the self.

We explored how the nervous system mobilizes under threat, how activation and dissociation emerge as survival strategies, and how regulation skills gradually expand the window of tolerance. That work established an essential foundation: the growing ability to remain present within one's own nervous system without becoming overwhelmed or fragmented.

But stabilization is not the end of healing. It is the beginning. Human nervous systems do not develop in isolation. They organize in relationship. And because they organize in relationship, they also heal in relationship.

This brings us to Stage Two of recovery: relational regulation.

If Stage One focused primarily on creating safety within the self, Stage Two widens outward into the interpersonal world. Here we begin exploring how attachment experiences shape autonomic regulation, emotional expectations, relational reflexes, and the nervous system's understanding of safety itself.

Trauma does not only alter how we feel internally.

It alters how we experience proximity, dependence, vulnerability, trust, conflict, and connection.

Stage Two therefore asks a deeper question: What happens to the nervous system when safety itself becomes relationally uncertain?

The Relational Nervous System

One of the most important discoveries in developmental neuroscience is that the human nervous system is profoundly relational from the very beginning of life.

In the late twentieth century, researchers studying Romanian orphanages observed something deeply sobering. Infants raised in conditions of severe emotional deprivation — despite receiving food, shelter, and basic physical care — demonstrated profound impairments in emotional, cognitive, relational, and physiological development. Later brain imaging studies revealed altered neural integration in regions associated with regulation, emotional processing, and social engagement.

The implications were enormous. Human beings are not biologically designed to mature alone.

From birth onward, infants depend on caregivers to regulate overwhelming internal states. A newborn cannot independently calm distress, organize emotion, regulate activation, or restore physiological equilibrium. The infant nervous system relies upon another nervous system for stabilization.

This process is known as co-regulation.

A caregiver's voice, facial expression, touch, eye contact, pacing, and emotional presence all influence the developing autonomic nervous system of the child. Through thousands of repeated interactions — being soothed when distressed, mirrored when joyful, comforted when frightened, repaired after rupture — the child gradually internalizes patterns of safety and regulation.

These experiences become encoded not only psychologically, but physiologically. Over time, the nervous system develops expectations about:

- whether distress will be soothed
- whether connection feels safe
- whether needs will be met
- whether vulnerability increases danger
- whether closeness leads to stability or pain

These expectations eventually organize into attachment patterns.

Attachment is often discussed as though it were merely a psychological theory.

In reality, attachment is deeply biological. It is a survival system embedded within the autonomic nervous system itself.

Proximity to safe caregivers reduces cortisol, stabilizes heart rate, increases vagal tone, and activates the social engagement system described within polyvagal theory. The nervous system literally organizes around relational experience.

Secure Attachment and the Development of Safety

Secure attachment does not emerge from perfect parenting. It emerges from sufficiently consistent repair.

All caregivers misattune at times. They become distracted, impatient, emotionally unavailable, stressed, or overwhelmed. What matters developmentally is not perfection, but the repeated restoration of connection after disruption.

The caregiver returns. They reconnect. They soothe.

Through this ongoing rhythm of rupture and repair, the child learns several foundational nervous-system truths:

Distress can be survived. Connection restores regulation. Needs are tolerable. Closeness is not inherently dangerous.

Conflict does not automatically lead to abandonment.

Over time, these experiences become embodied expectations.

By adulthood, individuals with relatively secure attachment often demonstrate greater flexibility in both intimacy and autonomy. Their nervous systems can generally tolerate emotional closeness without panic and separation without collapse. They are more capable of remaining regulated during conflict, seeking support when distressed, and maintaining connection during emotional strain.

Importantly, this does not mean securely attached individuals never become activated.

It means their nervous systems have greater confidence that regulation and repair are possible.

When Regulation Develops Under Strain

But many nervous systems developed under very different conditions.

When caregiving environments are inconsistent, frightening, emotionally unavailable, intrusive, rejecting, or chaotic, the nervous system adapts accordingly.

Attachment patterns are therefore not personality types. They are adaptive regulation strategies.

Consider anxious attachment. When caregiving is inconsistent — emotionally available at times and withdrawn at others — the nervous system learns vigilance. The sympathetic system becomes highly sensitive to signs of relational distance or disconnection. Small changes in tone, responsiveness, facial expression, or proximity begin feeling emotionally significant.

The adult nervous system may become highly reactive to:

- delayed messages
- subtle shifts in mood
- perceived withdrawal
- emotional ambiguity
- uncertainty in connection

This is not simply "neediness." It is a nervous system trained to anticipate abandonment.

Avoidant attachment develops differently. When emotional needs are dismissed, minimized, criticized, or met with discomfort, the child often learns that vulnerability itself increases risk. Over time, attachment needs become suppressed. Emotional distancing becomes protective. The nervous system reduces overt dependency in order to preserve safety.

As adults, these individuals may appear highly self-reliant and independent while simultaneously struggling with vulnerability, emotional intimacy, or sustained closeness.

Their nervous systems learned: Need creates danger.

Distance creates safety.

Disorganized attachment develops under even more destabilizing conditions — environments in which the caregiver becomes both the source of comfort and the source of fear. Here the nervous system receives profoundly conflicting signals. The attachment system simultaneously activates approach and avoidance responses.

The result is often relational chaos internally:

- longing mixed with fear
- closeness mixed with panic
- pursuit followed by withdrawal
- activation followed by collapse

Relationships may feel intensely compelling and profoundly destabilizing at the same time.

In every attachment style, the pattern reflects adaptation. The child did not consciously choose these strategies. The nervous system organized around survival.

Attachment Patterns Are Not Fixed Identities

This is one of the most hopeful discoveries in modern attachment research. Attachment patterns are not permanent identities. They are dynamic nervous system organizations shaped through repeated relational experience.

Research on earned secure attachment demonstrates that adults can gradually reorganize attachment patterns through consistent corrective relational experiences over time. This reorganization may emerge through the steady attunement of therapy, emotionally safe partnerships, secure friendships, supportive communities, spiritual connection, and repeated experiences of co-regulation in which distress is met with calm presence rather than abandonment or rejection.

Over time, the nervous system begins updating its expectations about connection. It learns through repetition. When vulnerability is consistently met with safety, responsiveness, and repair, the body slowly begins to loosen the defensive strategies that were once necessary for survival.

When distress is consistently met with steadiness rather than abandonment, the brain updates its expectations. When vulnerability is met with responsiveness rather than dismissal, defensive withdrawal gradually softens. When relational rupture is followed by repair, the nervous system begins learning that conflict does not inevitably threaten survival.

Stage Two of the Relational Nervous System Integration Model™ therefore focuses not on changing personality, but on reorganizing relational expectation at the level of the nervous system itself.

The body gradually learns something new: connection can be safe.

The Bridge from Self-Regulation to Co-Regulation

Stage One prepared us for this work.

Without stabilization capacity, relational triggers often overwhelm the nervous system too quickly for meaningful repair to occur. But once basic regulation skills are established, individuals can begin observing how their nervous systems organize in proximity to other people.

With stabilization capacity in place, individuals can begin noticing how their nervous systems organize in proximity to others. Some move anxiously toward reassurance and closeness. Others withdraw quickly when emotional intensity rises. Some become hypervigilant during conflict, carefully scanning tone, facial expression, or subtle shifts in mood for signs of danger. Others shut down emotionally when intimacy deepens, while some oscillate unpredictably between longing for connection and fearing it at the same time.

These patterns are not moral failures.

They are protective choreography learned through earlier relational experience.

Healing at this stage therefore involves two parallel developmental processes unfolding together: strengthening internal regulation while also participating in relationships that foster safe co-regulation. Over time, repeated experiences of relational steadiness begin teaching the nervous system something new. Connection does not always lead to danger. Vulnerability does not always lead to abandonment. Conflict does not always end in rupture.

As we move forward, we will explore how attachment patterns shape adult intimacy, emotional activation, vulnerability, conflict, and connection — and how earned security develops gradually through repeated relational safety.

The nervous system was shaped in relationship.

It will be reshaped there as well.

Chapter 8 - Rewiring the Relational Brain

"Secure attachment is not something we are born with or without. It is something we can build, through relationships that are safe enough and consistent enough for the nervous system to learn a new pattern." — Daniel J. Siegel

In the previous chapter, we explored how attachment patterns organize the nervous system around expectations of safety, connection, vulnerability, and protection. We examined how anxious, avoidant, and disorganized attachment strategies emerge not as personality flaws, but as adaptive regulatory responses shaped through repeated relational experience.

But an essential question naturally follows: Are these patterns fixed?

For many years, attachment was viewed as largely determined in childhood. Early relational environments were thought to establish relatively stable attachment structures that persisted throughout adult life. Contemporary attachment research, however, paints a far more hopeful picture.

Many adults who grew up in insecure relational environments later develop secure functioning over time.

Developmental researchers refer to this process as earned secure attachment.

Security, in these cases, was not inherited through early consistency. It was gradually constructed through corrective relational experience.

And importantly, this transformation is not merely psychological. It is neurobiological.

Within Stage Two of the Relational Nervous System Integration Model™, earned security represents one of the nervous system's most profound forms of reorganization. The brain slowly updates its predictions about connection, safety, vulnerability, and repair through repeated relational experiences that contradict earlier expectations of danger.

The nervous system learns a new pattern.

Attachment as a Neural Blueprint

Attachment is far more than a relational style or interpersonal preference. It is a biologically organized regulatory system designed to maintain survival and emotional equilibrium within relationships.

From infancy onward, the developing brain constructs what attachment theorists refer to as internal working models — implicit neural templates that organize expectations about safety, availability, responsiveness, rejection, abandonment, closeness, and self-worth. These models form long before language is fully developed. They emerge through repeated cycles of distress, regulation, rupture, and repair.

When caregivers respond consistently and reconnect reliably after disruption, the infant nervous system experiences activation followed by soothing. Over time, the brain begins encoding an expectation: distress can be survived in connection.

But when caregiving environments are inconsistent, frightening, intrusive, emotionally absent, or unpredictable, the nervous system encodes a very different relational forecast. Closeness may begin feeling dangerous. Vulnerability may become associated with shame, engulfment, rejection, or abandonment.

These experiences do not remain merely emotional memories. They shape neural development itself.

Research in interpersonal neurobiology suggests that attachment experiences influence the development and integration of several key neural systems, including the amygdala's threat sensitivity, the anterior cingulate cortex's processing of social pain, the insula's interoceptive awareness, and the regulatory pathways linking the prefrontal cortex and limbic system. In relatively secure attachment, communication between regulatory cortical regions and emotional centers tends to be more integrated, allowing emotional activation to be modulated rather than amplified. In insecure attachment, by contrast, threat systems often become hypersensitive while emotionally suppressive patterns become chronically reinforced.

Attachment, at its core, is the nervous system's best prediction about what connection will cost.

Earned security develops when that prediction gradually changes.

The Brain as a Prediction Engine

Modern neuroscience increasingly conceptualizes the brain not simply as a reactive organ, but as a predictive one.

Rather than waiting passively for experience to occur, the nervous system continuously generates forecasts based on prior relational learning. Attachment patterns therefore function as predictive models organizing perception, emotional interpretation, and autonomic response.

If early relational experiences taught the nervous system that closeness leads to abandonment, humiliation, engulfment, unpredictability, or emotional pain, then ambiguous relational cues will automatically be filtered through those expectations.

An unanswered text message may activate neural circuitry originally shaped by earlier experiences of rejection or emotional inconsistency. A subtle shift in tone may trigger threat responses long before conscious reasoning evaluates the situation rationally. As affective neuroscience repeatedly demonstrates, emotional activation frequently precedes conscious interpretation.

This helps explain why attachment reactions often feel immediate, involuntary, and disproportionate.

The nervous system is not reacting only to the present moment. It is reacting to predictions shaped by the past.

Earned secure attachment involves the gradual updating of those predictions.

Insight alone is rarely sufficient. The nervous system requires lived contradiction.

When abandonment is expected but steadiness occurs, a prediction error is introduced. When vulnerability is met with responsiveness rather than rejection, older emotional forecasts begin weakening. Research on memory reconsolidation suggests that when emotional networks become activated while simultaneously paired with new corrective experience, the neural encoding itself can reorganize.

Gradually, the old prediction that connection equals danger begins yielding to a new one:

Connection can be safe.

Integration and Neural Coherence

One of the hallmarks of earned secure attachment is increasing neural integration.

Daniel J. Siegel describes integration as the linking of differentiated neural systems into flexible coordination. Neuroimaging research suggests that securely attached adults often demonstrate stronger functional connectivity between regulatory cortical regions and emotional centers such as the amygdala.

In practical terms, this means emotional activation can occur without overwhelming the individual's regulatory capacity.

In anxious attachment, sympathetic activation may escalate rapidly, producing urgency, rumination, hypervigilance, and fear of abandonment. In avoidant organization, emotional suppression and dorsal vagal withdrawal may reduce conscious access to vulnerability and need.

Earned security does not eliminate these systems entirely. Rather, it increases flexibility within them.

Emotions can arise without flooding the individual. Conflict can occur without catastrophic assumptions. Vulnerability can feel uncomfortable without triggering collapse or disconnection.

Security is not the absence of activation.

It is the presence of regulation within activation.

Autonomic Flexibility and Relational Presence

Polyvagal theory further illuminates this transformation.

The ventral vagal system supports social engagement, facial expressivity, vocal modulation, emotional reciprocity, and physiological calm during connection. Research involving heart rate variability increasingly suggests that greater vagal flexibility correlates with emotional regulation, relational resilience, and adaptive recovery from stress.

Adults developing earned security often gradually strengthen this autonomic flexibility over time.

Their nervous systems become increasingly capable of tolerating relational stress while remaining emotionally engaged rather than immediately shifting into pursuit, shutdown, withdrawal, or fragmentation.

They pause more often. They reflect more effectively. They remain present longer during emotional intensity.

This shift is not simply cognitive intention. It is physiological learning.

Memory Reconsolidation and Relational Repair

Attachment healing frequently unfolds through repeated cycles of rupture and repair.

Research in psychotherapy and attachment science consistently highlights repair as one of the primary mechanisms through which security develops. When misunderstandings occur and are later addressed with clarity, emotional honesty, accountability, and warmth, the nervous system receives new relational data.

The emotional memory network temporarily destabilizes and becomes available for updating.

This process — often referred to as memory reconsolidation — allows relational expectations to gradually reorganize at the neural level. The individual does not merely decide intellectually to trust differently.

The body begins anticipating differently. Over time, these micro-experiences accumulate. The internal working model slowly changes.

Therapy often becomes one structured environment in which this process unfolds. Predictable boundaries, consistent attunement, relational steadiness, and transparent repair create conditions in which the nervous system can safely experiment with new relational expectations.

Initially, regulation is co-created. The therapist's nervous system functions as external scaffolding.

Gradually, the client internalizes that steadiness. The space between trigger and reaction lengthens. Emotional waves become more tolerable. Vulnerability becomes less threatening.

This is not dependency. It is developmental neurobiology.

A Clinical Illustration

Daniel entered therapy describing himself as "emotionally volatile."

Raised in an environment marked by unpredictability and emotional inconsistency, he oscillated between intense pursuit of closeness and abrupt emotional withdrawal. Small moments of perceived misunderstanding frequently triggered shame, panic, or detachment.

In earlier periods of his life, these relational ruptures typically ended in disconnection.

But in therapy, we slowed the process down.

We named the activation directly. We tracked the nervous system shifts. We repaired misunderstandings explicitly rather than bypassing them.

Months later, Daniel described a disagreement with his partner in which something new occurred.

"My body expected to disappear," he said quietly, "but it didn't."

That subtle moment reflected profound nervous system reorganization.

Earned secure attachment is rarely dramatic. More often, it emerges through increasing flexibility — the growing ability to remain present longer during activation, recover more quickly after rupture, tolerate vulnerability more fully, and maintain connection without immediately collapsing into pursuit or withdrawal.

Old circuits may still activate under stress. But the secure pathway becomes increasingly accessible.

Security is not about erasing history. It is about reorganizing it.

From Relational Safety to Embodied Memory

As we move forward in the Relational Nervous System Integration Model™, we now widen the lens further.

Attachment does not live only within romantic relationships or family systems. It lives within the nervous system's broader expectations of safety itself.

Those expectations travel with us everywhere — into workplaces, conflict, solitude, authority structures, and environments involving vulnerability or loss of control.

Few environments activate attachment and survival circuitry more quickly than medical settings. In those moments, the body is positioned, evaluated, touched, examined, and sometimes overruled. Predictability narrows. Autonomy shifts outward. The nervous system must rapidly determine whether safety is present.

For individuals whose early experiences linked vulnerability with helplessness, shame, or powerlessness, even routine healthcare encounters may activate deeply encoded relational memory.

If this chapter explored how attachment becomes organized within the relational brain, the next chapter will examine how those attachment patterns surface within the body itself — particularly in environments where vulnerability becomes unavoidable.

The nervous system remembers.

And it can also relearn.

Chapter 9 - Trauma in Healthcare

"The body keeps the score: if the memory of trauma is encoded in the viscera, the heart, and the immune system, then it must be healed there as well." — Bessel van der Kolk

In the previous chapter, we explored how attachment patterns shape the nervous system's expectations about safety, vulnerability, repair, and connection. We examined how earned secure attachment gradually reorganizes the brain's predictive models through repeated corrective relational experience, allowing the nervous system to update its expectations about closeness and trust.

But attachment does not live only inside relationships. It also lives inside the body.

The nervous system carries its relational expectations into physical environments, particularly those involving vulnerability, uncertainty, exposure, or diminished control. Few settings activate these survival systems more quickly than healthcare environments.

For some individuals, the scent of disinfectant, the brightness of fluorescent lighting, the sound of monitors, hurried footsteps, medical equipment, or unfamiliar voices remain emotionally neutral. For others, those same stimuli evoke immediate physiological activation: a racing heart, shallow breathing, dizziness, muscular tension, irritability, emotional shutdown, or a diffuse sense of impending danger that seems disproportionate to the situation itself.

What appears externally as anxiety is often something far more specific. The nervous system is retrieving previously encoded relational memory associated with vulnerability, helplessness, or fear.

This is where Stage Two of the Relational Nervous System Integration Model™ becomes increasingly visible. After the stabilization work developed in Stage One and the relational awareness cultivated through attachment work, individuals begin recognizing that activation is not random. It is patterned, learned, and stored within the nervous system in ways that frequently operate outside conscious awareness.

Healthcare environments often reveal those patterns with remarkable clarity.

The Body as an Archive

Medical trauma does not always emerge from dramatic emergencies or catastrophic procedures. Often it develops quietly through experiences that, from the outside, may appear relatively ordinary: a child restrained during a frightening procedure, a patient receiving devastating news alone, an invasive examination performed without emotional preparation, or a vulnerable person feeling dismissed, powerless, or emotionally abandoned during moments of fear or pain.

In experiences such as these, the body may encode helplessness long before the mind possesses the language necessary to organize the event coherently.

This is why trauma survivors so often say, “I know I’m safe now, but my body doesn’t believe it.”

That statement captures one of the central realities of trauma recovery: the distinction between cognitive understanding and implicit memory. Trauma does not persist because individuals fail to think rationally about the past. It persists because the nervous system has stored threat procedurally, at the level of autonomic expectation and bodily prediction.

Research involving implicit memory, autonomic conditioning, and affective neuroscience increasingly suggests that sensory cues such as lighting, smell, vocal tone, physical positioning, touch, or environmental atmosphere can reactivate stored threat responses long before conscious interpretation occurs. The amygdala rapidly detects pattern similarity before the cortex has fully evaluated present context. The body therefore reacts first, while conscious explanation arrives later.

From the perspective of the nervous system, this makes profound sense. The brain is designed to prioritize survival, not accuracy. If previous experiences associated vulnerability with helplessness or danger, the nervous system learns to anticipate threat whenever similar sensory conditions arise again.

A Clinical Illustration

Jonathan, a thirty-four-year-old teacher, sought therapy after nearly fainting during a routine blood draw. He described sudden dizziness, overwhelming panic, blurred vision, and an intense urge to escape, followed almost immediately by embarrassment and self-criticism.

At first, the reaction seemed confusing even to him. "It was just bloodwork," he repeated, unable to understand why his body reacted with such intensity.

As we explored his history more carefully, earlier experiences gradually surfaced. During childhood, Jonathan had spent several weeks hospitalized for a severe infection. He remembered waking disoriented after procedures, crying alone, and feeling separated from his parents during frightening medical interventions. Although many details remained vague, the emotional tone of helplessness and disorientation remained strongly encoded within his nervous system.

The adult clinic environment unconsciously replicated many of the same sensory conditions: the antiseptic scent, the latex gloves, the bright overhead lighting, the positioning of the body, and the loss of control. His reaction was not irrational. It was coherent within the nervous system's stored archive of vulnerability.

Once this pattern was named, something important shifted. Shame softened. The experience moved from "What is wrong with me?" to "My body is protecting me using old information."

That reframing often represents one of the earliest and most important movements within Stage Two healing. Individuals begin recognizing their symptoms not as evidence of weakness or defectiveness, but as adaptive protective responses shaped through earlier experience.

Why Healthcare Settings Activate the Nervous System

Healthcare environments uniquely combine several elements that intensify nervous system vulnerability.

First, they frequently involve a temporary surrender of control. The body becomes subject to instruction, examination, positioning, touch, and procedural intervention. Even within fully consensual medical care, the nervous system must still process reduced autonomy and increased dependency upon external authority.

Second, these environments often involve high levels of sensory intensity. Bright lighting, unfamiliar equipment, cold rooms, physical discomfort, hurried speech, alarms, exposure of the body, and uncertainty all contribute to heightened autonomic activation.

Third, previous relational memory may become attached to these experiences. If earlier moments of fear, helplessness, abandonment, shame, or powerlessness occurred within similar environments, the nervous system rapidly retrieves those emotional templates and applies them to the present moment.

None of this reflects pathology. It reflects predictive coding at work. The brain is attempting to prevent repetition of earlier harm by anticipating danger before conscious reasoning has fully evaluated the situation.

The nervous system is constantly asking: Have we been unsafe here before?

And if the answer encoded within implicit memory is yes, activation emerges automatically.

Interoception and Escalation Loops

Healthcare environments also tend to amplify interoception, or the awareness of internal bodily sensations. Heart rate becomes more noticeable. Muscle tension intensifies. Breathing feels shallower. Dizziness or nausea becomes alarming.

If these physiological sensations are interpreted as evidence of danger, a rapid escalation loop can develop. Heightened sensation produces fear. Fear increases autonomic activation. Increased activation intensifies bodily sensation further. Without awareness, the nervous system can quickly spiral into panic, shutdown, dissociation, or emotional overwhelm.

This is precisely where the stabilization capacities developed during Stage One become essential within Stage Two relational work. Orienting exercises, paced breathing, grounding, sensory awareness, and present-time attention interrupt the escalation cycle by helping the nervous system differentiate past activation from present reality.

Gradually, clients begin learning to recognize the difference between activation and catastrophe. That distinction may appear deceptively simple, but neurobiologically it represents a profound shift.

When repeated consistently alongside corrective experience, the nervous system slowly expands its capacity to remain present within previously triggering environments.

A Second Illustration

Linda, a fifty-eight-year-old cancer survivor, avoided follow-up screenings for years after completing treatment. She described feeling as though "the walls close in" the moment she entered the clinic.

Importantly, her trauma did not emerge from overt medical mistreatment. It developed through prolonged uncertainty during her original diagnosis: waiting alone for results, imagining worst-case scenarios in silence, and carrying overwhelming fear without sufficient relational support.

Over time, the clinic environment itself became paired with anticipatory dread. Her nervous system no longer interpreted the building neutrally. It interpreted it as threat.

Through stabilization work, we gradually developed a pre-appointment ritual designed to increase regulation and predictability. Before entering the clinic, Linda practiced paced breathing in the parking lot. Inside the building, she intentionally oriented visually to calming environmental cues. She brought a trusted friend for co-regulation and support, and afterward she intentionally engaged in restorative activities that signaled completion and safety to the nervous system.

Gradually, the environment lost some of its singular threat coding. The memory remained, but the nervous system's forecast slowly changed. What once triggered overwhelming collapse became increasingly tolerable.

This is one of the most important principles in trauma recovery: healing does not necessarily erase memory. It reorganizes the nervous system's relationship to memory.

Reclaiming Agency

Recovery from medical trauma is not primarily about eliminating fear. It is about restoring agency within experiences that once felt overwhelming or powerless.

Trauma often leaves individuals feeling trapped inside circumstances they could not influence, interrupt, or escape. Healing therefore involves helping the nervous system experience present-day vulnerability differently. Patients can ask providers to slow down. They can request step-by-step explanations, establish consent-based touch, pause procedures, bring supportive people into appointments, ask questions openly, and advocate for themselves directly.

Although these actions may appear small externally, they carry profound neurobiological significance. Each successful act of agency introduces new data into the nervous system. Vulnerability gradually becomes experienced as collaborative rather than imposed.

Within Stage Two work, therapy often involves rehearsing these moments beforehand. The nervous system must not merely understand boundaries cognitively. It must experience successful boundary-setting physiologically.

That experience changes prediction.

From Vulnerability to Embodied Healing

As individuals begin recognizing healthcare activation as stored relational memory, another important shift gradually occurs. The environment itself stops becoming the primary enemy. Attention instead turns toward understanding the nervous system's patterned responses with greater compassion and clarity.

The goal is not perfect calm. The goal is increased capacity.

Over time, clinics that once triggered collapse become manageable. Procedures that once felt unbearable become tolerable. The nervous system gradually learns differentiation between then and now, between past helplessness and present agency, between stored memory and immediate danger.

This differentiation becomes one of the central bridges between attachment healing and embodied healing.

And it prepares us for the next developmental movement within the Relational Nervous System Integration Model™.

Because trauma is not stored only in environments or relationships. It is also carried in posture, muscle tension, breathing patterns, movement, autonomic reflexes, and the body itself.

In the next chapter, we turn more fully toward somatic experience, exploring how trauma reshapes physiology and how intentional engagement with the body becomes an essential pathway toward deeper regulation and integration.

The nervous system remembers.

But fortunately, it also updates.

Chapter 10 - The Body Remembers: Implicit Memory

"You cannot solve a problem until you understand it." — Albert Einstein

In the previous chapter, we explored how healthcare environments can activate stored relational memory and how the nervous system responds not only to present reality, but to earlier patterns encoded in sensory and procedural memory. We saw that trauma frequently lives beneath conscious awareness, emerging through bodily activation long before the thinking mind fully understands what is happening.

In this chapter, we move more deeply into the body itself.

If attachment shapes expectation and environments trigger activation, the body becomes the place where those patterns are carried forward physiologically. Trauma is not remembered only as story. It is also organized as posture, muscle tension, breathing patterns, reflexive movement, autonomic bias, and embodied anticipation.

The body does not narrate experience in the way the conscious mind does. It prepares for it.

This marks an important developmental deepening within the *Relational Nervous System Integration Model™*. Earlier stages focused on stabilization, regulation, attachment, and relational safety. Now we begin examining how traumatic experience becomes embedded within physiology itself, and how integration requires more than cognitive insight alone. The nervous system must gradually learn, through embodied experience, that the danger it once organized around is no longer occurring in the present moment.

Trauma as Procedural Memory

Modern neuroscience distinguishes between explicit memory and implicit memory. Explicit memory refers to the narrative experiences we can consciously recall and describe. Implicit memory, by contrast, includes emotional learning, procedural conditioning, autonomic responses, bodily habits, and sensory associations that operate largely outside conscious awareness.

Trauma frequently bypasses explicit narrative storage and becomes encoded within these implicit systems instead.

When overwhelming threat exceeds the nervous system's regulatory capacity, the brain prioritizes survival over coherent autobiographical organization. The hippocampus, which helps organize memory into narrative sequence and context, may become less integrated during acute stress, while subcortical systems associated with threat detection and survival response become increasingly dominant.

As trauma researchers such as Bessel van der Kolk have repeatedly emphasized, the body "keeps the score" not metaphorically, but physiologically.

A raised voice may trigger shoulder tension before conscious awareness recognizes fear. A closed door may quicken breathing. Certain facial expressions, postures, tones of voice, or interpersonal dynamics may evoke collapse, vigilance, or withdrawal automatically.

These reactions are not consciously chosen.

They are predictive responses generated by nervous system circuitry attempting to prevent recurrence of earlier harm.

This is why an important shift begins occurring during Stage Two integration. Individuals gradually move away from asking only, "Why do I feel this way?" and begin asking a deeper question:

"What is my nervous system preparing for?"

That question changes the entire framework of healing. Symptoms begin making sense not as evidence of defectiveness, but as organized survival adaptations.

The Physiology of Protection

When threat is perceived, the autonomic nervous system shifts outside the window of tolerance and mobilizes for protection.

Sympathetic activation increases heart rate, tightens musculature, narrows attention, and prepares the body for action through fight or flight responses. If escape or effective action no longer appears possible, the nervous system may instead shift toward dorsal vagal immobilization, producing slowing, collapse, emotional numbing, exhaustion, dissociation, or disconnection.

Both responses are adaptive.

The difficulty emerges when these physiological patterns persist long after the original threat has ended. The nervous system becomes chronically organized around protection rather than flexibility. Muscles remain guarded. Breathing stays constricted. Sleep becomes disrupted. Digestive systems become dysregulated. Fatigue, chronic pain, migraines, hypervigilance, or emotional shutdown may all reflect unresolved autonomic cycling that the body no longer knows how to complete.

The nervous system continues preparing for danger even when the environment itself is relatively safe.

Integration does not eliminate these protective systems. It restores flexibility and choice within them. The goal is not to eradicate activation, but to help the body recognize when protection is no longer necessary.

A Clinical Illustration

Elena came to therapy describing chronic neck pain and persistent fatigue. Like many individuals struggling with long-standing physical symptoms, she initially assumed the cause was entirely orthopedic or muscular.

Yet as we began tracking her physiology during emotionally significant moments in session, a consistent pattern emerged. Whenever conflict or criticism entered the conversation, her shoulders subtly rose, her breathing shortened, and her voice became quieter and less expressive.

Over time, it became clear that her body had learned an implicit survival strategy long before she consciously recognized it.

As a child, visibility frequently led to criticism and emotional invalidation. Her nervous system adapted by minimizing presence. Her body learned to contract before her conscious mind even formed words.

The neck pain was not imagined. It was patterned contraction.

Through gradual somatic awareness, relational safety, breath work, and gentle experimentation with posture and movement, Elena slowly began exploring different physiological possibilities. She practiced sitting upright while remaining emotionally present.

She noticed the urge to collapse inward and gently interrupted it. She experimented with allowing breath to deepen during difficult conversations rather than unconsciously constricting.

The work unfolded slowly, but over time the chronic tension began easing.

Her body was updating its prediction.

Interoception and Integration

Stage Two integration relies heavily upon interoception, the ability to perceive and interpret internal bodily states.

Research on interoception suggests that individuals with trauma histories frequently develop one of two broad adaptations. Some become highly sensitive to internal sensations, monitoring bodily shifts continuously and often interpreting them as evidence of danger. Others become significantly disconnected from bodily awareness altogether, experiencing numbness, disembodiment, or difficulty identifying internal states.

Both patterns reflect adaptation.

Hyperawareness may create escalating anxiety loops, while disconnection may reduce access to emotional and physiological information necessary for regulation.

The goal of integration is not to intensify sensation, but to cultivate tolerable awareness.

This often begins quite simply: noticing tension in the jaw, sensing the movement of breath, recognizing tightening in the shoulders, feeling the support of the floor beneath the feet, or observing subtle physiological shifts without immediately interpreting them as catastrophe.

When awareness becomes paired with regulation through breathing, grounding, orientation, movement, and relational safety, the nervous system gradually experiences something profoundly important: sensation without overwhelm.

This is one of the central mechanisms of integration. The body learns that activation, discomfort, emotion, and physiological sensation can exist without automatically requiring collapse, panic, or dissociation.

Posture, Movement, and Memory

Trauma becomes encoded not only through emotional activation, but also through inhibited movement and interrupted defensive responses.

In the natural world, animals often discharge survival energy through shaking, running, vocalizing, or physical movement after threat has passed. Human beings, however, frequently suppress these impulses due to social conditioning, fear, shame, or ongoing danger.

As a result, incomplete defensive responses may remain stored physiologically as chronic muscular holding patterns, restricted breathing, frozen posture, or inhibited movement.

Somatic therapies increasingly suggest that small, carefully titrated movements can help the nervous system complete previously interrupted survival sequences. A subtle turning movement, a gentle pushing motion, grounding through the legs, or the experience of taking up slightly more physical space may introduce new procedural information into the body.

Importantly, this process does not require dramatic catharsis or emotional flooding. In fact, overwhelming activation often disrupts integration rather than facilitating it.

Healing tends to occur through gradual experimentation within the window of tolerance, where the nervous system can remain sufficiently regulated while encountering new embodied experiences.

Small movements can update very large predictions.

Differentiating Then from Now

One of the central developmental tasks of Stage Two involves differentiation.

The nervous system must gradually learn the distinction between past threat and present safety.

This learning cannot occur through logic alone. It emerges through repeated embodied experiences in which activation is present while danger is absent.

For example, a client may notice anxiety arising during disagreement with a partner. Historically, conflict may have predicted humiliation, abandonment, volatility, or emotional collapse. But instead of withdrawing automatically, the individual remains present while breathing slowly, observing facial expression, listening carefully to tone of voice, and recognizing the absence of immediate threat.

Experiences such as these gradually strengthen neural pathways associated with present-time evaluation rather than automatic survival prediction.

Over time, the body begins expecting safety more often than catastrophe.

This is not denial of the past.

It is the nervous system learning flexibility.

The Role of Relational Safety

Although Stage Two involves body-level integration, the process remains fundamentally relational.

Secure attachment experiences continue providing corrective feedback to the nervous system. When another regulated human being remains emotionally steady during our activation, mirror neuron systems, autonomic pathways, and social engagement circuitry all contribute to down-regulation and increased physiological safety.

This is one reason therapeutic presence matters so profoundly. It is also why emotionally safe relationships accelerate integration. The nervous system updates most effectively in the context of regulated connection.

Stage One built capacity for stabilization and regulation. Stage Two gradually builds flexibility. The goal is not eliminating activation entirely, but increasing the ability to experience activation without losing agency, connection, or self-awareness.

As integration deepens, individuals often begin noticing subtle but meaningful changes. Tension releases more quickly. Conflict feels less catastrophic. Recovery after activation becomes shorter. Physical symptoms soften. Emotional flexibility expands.

The body is no longer fighting itself with the same intensity. It is learning.

And as embodied integration strengthens, another question naturally begins to emerge.

If trauma shapes physiology, relationships, and nervous system expectation, what happens when it begins shaping identity itself — the stories individuals carry about who they are, what they deserve, and how they understand their own lives?

In the next chapter, we turn toward that inner narrative landscape, exploring how trauma influences self-perception, meaning-making, and identity formation, and how integration continues unfolding at the level of the self.

The nervous system prepares.

But it can also transform.

Chapter 11 - Reclaiming Identity After Trauma

"Recovery can take place only within the context of relationships; it cannot occur in isolation."— Judith Herman

As we have seen throughout the previous chapters, trauma shapes far more than emotional experience alone. It influences posture, breathing patterns, autonomic activation, relational expectations, and the nervous system's ongoing anticipation of safety or danger. Over time, however, these repeated physiological and relational experiences begin organizing something even deeper: the way individuals understand themselves.

This marks an important developmental movement within the Relational Nervous System Integration Model™. Earlier stages focused on stabilization, regulation, attachment, embodied awareness, and relational safety. But trauma does not only dysregulate the nervous system. It also reorganizes meaning. And meaning, repeated often enough, gradually becomes identity.

Trauma therefore changes more than how people feel. It changes the story they carry about who they are.

A child who grows up walking on eggshells, constantly scanning tone of voice, facial expression, and subtle emotional shifts for signs of danger, is adapting intelligently to an unpredictable environment. Hypervigilance may genuinely increase safety within the home. But over time, those protective physiological responses often crystallize into identity-level conclusions. The child who survives through vigilance may later believe, "I am too sensitive." The child who survives through emotional suppression may conclude, "I do not have needs." The child who survives by preventing conflict may quietly organize around the belief, "I am responsible for everyone else's feelings."

These conclusions rarely emerge through deliberate reasoning. They develop through repeated embodied experience. The brain continuously updates its internal model of reality based on patterns of survival, attachment, threat, and regulation. When experiences consistently communicate unpredictability, criticism, conditional love, abandonment, or emotional danger, the nervous system gradually constructs narratives that explain those experiences coherently. Eventually, those narratives stop feeling like interpretations and begin feeling like identity itself.

Research in neuroscience increasingly suggests that autobiographical memory and self-representation are closely linked through networks involving the medial prefrontal cortex, hippocampus, and default mode network. When trauma fragments memory and disrupts emotional integration, coherence of self may fragment as well. Integration therefore requires more than calming the nervous system. It requires restoring continuity within the story of the self.

One of the most important shifts in trauma recovery occurs when identity distortions are reframed not as character flaws, but as adaptive survival strategies. The invisible child was often protecting themselves from criticism or intrusion. The overachiever may have been securing belonging and safety through performance. The caretaker may have been preventing chaos. The emotionally numb individual may have been surviving overwhelm.

Viewed through this lens, trauma-based identities begin making sense.

Stage Two integration therefore invites a different kind of inquiry. Rather than asking, "What is wrong with me?" individuals gradually begin asking more compassionate and developmentally accurate questions: What was this strategy protecting me from? What did it help me survive? What did it cost me? And what do I need now that the original danger is no longer present?

Questions such as these begin shifting the nervous system away from shame and toward understanding. The goal is not to erase earlier adaptations, but to recognize them as intelligent responses that may no longer be necessary in their original form.

A Clinical Illustration

When David first entered therapy, he described himself as "emotionally defective." He struggled in relationships, avoided vulnerability, and experienced a chronic sense of emotional detachment from both himself and other people. As we explored his developmental history, however, a different story gradually emerged.

David had grown up in a household where emotional expression was mocked and vulnerability was met with contempt. Anger was tolerated. Tenderness was not. His nervous system adapted accordingly. Withdrawal became protective.

Over time, that withdrawal stopped feeling like a strategy and became incorporated into identity itself: "I am not emotional. I am distant. I do not connect the way other people do."

But his body told a more complicated story. Whenever he spoke about meaningful relationships, his jaw tightened, his breathing shortened, and subtle tension moved through his shoulders and chest. The detachment was not evidence of emotional absence. It was evidence of protective inhibition.

As David gradually learned to regulate his nervous system, tolerate greater emotional presence, and experiment with small disclosures inside safe relationships, a different identity slowly began emerging. He was not emotionally defective. He was emotionally guarded and learning safety.

That shift may appear subtle linguistically, but neurobiologically it represented profound reorganization. Identity-level integration had begun.

Trauma researchers such as Ronnie Janoff-Bulman have described how traumatic experience can shatter core assumptions individuals hold about themselves and the world around them. Beliefs such as "I am safe," "People can be trusted," or "I am worthy" may become profoundly destabilized after repeated threat, humiliation, abandonment, or emotional violation.

The brain naturally attempts to restore coherence after disruption. Unfortunately, it often does so through self-blame. "If it was my fault, maybe I can prevent it next time."

Paradoxically, self-blame can temporarily feel safer than helplessness because it preserves an illusion of control. Over time, however, these explanations become integrated into identity and begin shaping emotional expectation, behavior, and self-perception.

Cognitive integration therefore involves gently examining and revising trauma-generated conclusions through lived experience rather than forced positive thinking. When someone expresses anger safely and remains connected, identity begins shifting. When a person sets a boundary without abandonment occurring, identity shifts. When mistakes no longer produce humiliation or rejection, the nervous system updates its expectations again.

Over time, the brain begins constructing a different narrative about both self and relationship.

Stage Two integration also involves rebuilding narrative coherence. This does not require repeatedly reliving traumatic events. Rather, it involves placing those experiences within a broader context of adaptation, survival, resilience, and meaning. Clients often move gradually from "I am broken" to "My nervous system adapted," or from "I am weak" to "I survived what overwhelmed me."

Narrative coherence restores dignity because it reconnects painful experience to context rather than shame.

Neuroimaging research increasingly suggests that when traumatic memory becomes integrated into coherent narrative form, activity within emotional reactivity centers decreases while prefrontal regulatory activity increases. In practical terms, the brain becomes better able to hold difficult experience without becoming overwhelmed by it.

But cognitive story alone is rarely sufficient. The narrative must become embodied.

One of the most common misunderstandings in trauma recovery involves attempting to change identity entirely through cognition. "If I think differently, I will feel differently." Yet as we have repeatedly seen throughout this model, the nervous system operates both top-down and bottom-up. Identity shifts become stable only when cognitive understanding becomes paired with embodied experience.

A person may intellectually understand that they are worthy of love while their body simultaneously collapses inward when receiving praise. Someone may consciously believe they deserve boundaries while physiologically panicking when attempting to express one. In these moments, the older survival identity remains active within the nervous system despite newer cognitive insight.

Integration therefore requires helping the body experience what the mind is beginning to understand. An individual learns to breathe steadily while expressing need, to remain physically upright while receiving appreciation, to stay emotionally present during closeness, and to tolerate visibility without collapsing into shame or withdrawal.

Over time, the nervous system gradually reorganizes around these repeated embodied experiences. The body begins believing what the mind is learning.

As integration deepens, individuals often begin experiencing greater internal flexibility. Rather than becoming fused with a single trauma-shaped identity, they begin recognizing complexity within themselves. Anxiety and competence can coexist. Strength and vulnerability can coexist. Independence and the need for connection can coexist.

This flexibility reflects increasing integration across emotional, cognitive, physiological, and relational systems that previously operated defensively and in isolation from one another. Identity becomes more dynamic and less organized around survival.

Within the Relational Nervous System Integration Model™, this represents an important developmental shift. Survival-based identity continually asks, "How do I avoid harm?" An increasingly integrated identity begins asking, "How do I live meaningfully?"

This transition rarely occurs dramatically or all at once. It unfolds gradually through repeated experiences of safety, reflection, embodiment, and relational repair. And as individuals begin recognizing that their adaptations were intelligent rather than defective, another realization often emerges.

The hypervigilant child may have developed profound intuition and sensitivity. The caretaker may have cultivated deep empathy. The overachiever may have developed discipline and perseverance. The withdrawn individual may have become observant, thoughtful, and reflective.

Trauma leaves scars, but it often leaves capacities as well. Integration involves reclaiming both honestly.

By this point in the journey, stabilization has strengthened regulation. Integration has restored increasing embodiment, relational flexibility, and identity coherence. The nervous system is no longer organized entirely around survival in the same way it once was.

As this shift deepens, something important begins happening. The work is no longer focused exclusively on reducing symptoms, managing activation, or understanding old patterns. The nervous system begins experiencing moments of steadiness, flexibility, creativity, and possibility that were previously unavailable. Reactivity softens. Awareness expands. Choice becomes more accessible.

Within the Relational Nervous System Integration Model™, this marks the transition into Stage Three: Expansion.

Expansion does not mean pain disappears or life suddenly becomes effortless. Rather, it means that increasing amounts of nervous system energy become available for growth rather than protection. Energy once devoted primarily to vigilance, emotional suppression, or survival forecasting begins redirecting toward meaning-making, creativity, intimacy, purpose, and forward movement.

At this stage, healing naturally begins touching areas that many trauma survivors initially do not recognize as trauma-related at all, including work, ambition, relationships, purpose, and money. Because money is never only about numbers. It is also about safety, freedom, identity, possibility, and the nervous system's relationship to stability and control.

And so we now turn toward a subject that quietly influences nearly every adult life: the emotional and physiological relationship we have with money.

Chapter 12 - The Weight of Financial Trauma

"The importance of money flows from it being a link between the present and the future." —John Maynard Keynes

Up to this point in the Relational Nervous System Integration Model™, we have focused primarily on stabilization and integration. We have explored how trauma shapes physiology, attachment, identity, embodiment, and the nervous system's ongoing anticipation of danger. As healing progresses, however, the work begins expanding beyond symptom reduction and survival management alone.

This marks the beginning of Stage Three: Expansion.

Expansion does not mean the absence of difficulty, uncertainty, or stress. Rather, it reflects a gradual widening of the nervous system's capacity to move beyond chronic protection and into increasing agency, creativity, intentionality, and forward movement. Energy that was once consumed by vigilance and survival forecasting slowly becomes available for building a life rather than merely enduring one.

One of the clearest places this developmental shift emerges is in our relationship with money.

Money is often discussed as though it were purely practical — a matter of budgets, debt, income, savings, retirement plans, and financial strategy. On the surface, it appears rational and objective. Numbers either add up or they do not.

Yet in the therapy room, money rarely feels neutral.

Behind financial decisions there is often something far more emotionally charged: fear, shame, longing, identity, control, freedom, and the nervous system's ongoing attempt to create safety in an uncertain world. Over time, money can quietly accumulate symbolic meaning far beyond economics alone. It may come to represent survival, worth, autonomy, belonging, stability, or failure — sometimes all at once.

When financial experiences become overwhelming or chronically stressful, the nervous system may begin organizing around them in ways that closely resemble other trauma patterns. This is what many clinicians and trauma researchers increasingly refer to as financial trauma.

Although financial trauma is not an official diagnostic category, the lived experience is unmistakable. It describes a pattern in which real or perceived financial threat leaves lasting emotional and physiological imprints within the nervous system: hypervigilance, chronic dread, avoidance, shame, impulsivity, or a persistent sense that safety could disappear at any moment.

In this state, money stops functioning merely as a resource.

It becomes a threat-detection system.

When Money Becomes a Nervous System Experience

It is common to assume that financial anxiety reflects poor planning, irresponsibility, or lack of discipline. Trauma science offers a far more compassionate and physiologically accurate lens.

The nervous system does not respond only to objective reality. It responds to perceived threat.

For some individuals, financial trauma begins suddenly through job loss, divorce, bankruptcy, medical crisis, business collapse, or overwhelming debt. For others, it develops gradually through years of instability, chronic scarcity, unpredictability, or emotional tension surrounding money inside the family system.

Research in stress physiology increasingly suggests that prolonged financial strain can shape brain and body patterns in ways remarkably similar to other forms of chronic threat exposure. When safety feels uncertain, the nervous system adapts accordingly.

Some individuals become highly vigilant, monitoring every dollar while living in constant anticipation of loss. Others move toward avoidance, finding themselves unable to open bills, review accounts, or discuss finances because the experience triggers overwhelming anxiety or shame. Still others oscillate between rigid financial control and impulsive spending as the nervous system attempts, imperfectly, to regulate itself behaviorally.

From the outside, these patterns may appear irrational or self-sabotaging.

From a nervous system perspective, they are deeply coherent. They are survival strategies organized around protection.

The Early Roots of Financial Identity

Financial trauma rarely begins in adulthood. Long before individuals manage money themselves, they absorb emotional lessons about safety, resources, and stability within the homes where they grow up.

Children learn not only what parents say about money, but how money feels inside the emotional atmosphere of the household. A home in which bills routinely trigger conflict, where scarcity feels chronic, or where financial conversations are saturated with secrecy, fear, shame, or unpredictability teaches the developing nervous system important lessons about survival.

Without consciously realizing it, the child's body begins mapping answers to questions they cannot yet articulate:

Are resources stable or fragile?

Is provision predictable or conditional?

Does money create calm or tension?

Even seemingly ordinary phrases such as "we can't afford that," "money doesn't grow on trees," or "people like us never get ahead" may become embedded as implicit beliefs that continue shaping adult behavior decades later.

What makes these financial narratives particularly powerful is that they often operate outside conscious awareness. Someone may achieve significant external success while internally feeling perpetually one step away from collapse. Another person may unconsciously restrict financial growth because expansion itself feels unfamiliar and therefore unsafe.

The nervous system remembers patterns long after external circumstances change.

When Financial Stress Reshapes Identity

Financial disruption often cuts deeper than the loss of money itself. It frequently destabilizes identity.

The provider begins questioning their worth. The fiercely independent person suddenly feels exposed and vulnerable. The high-performing professional confronts a frightening loss of predictability and control.

Trauma researchers sometimes describe this experience as a shattering of assumptions — a disruption of deeply held beliefs about competence, safety, stability, or the future.

Within financial trauma, the nervous system may gradually begin associating money not with possibility, but with danger. Decision-making narrows. Fear dominates imagination. Long-term planning becomes more difficult because the body remains oriented toward immediate survival rather than future-oriented thinking.

This helps explain why individuals under financial stress sometimes make decisions that appear irrational from the outside. When the nervous system senses threat, access to reflective thinking and strategic planning becomes biologically constrained. Survival processes take precedence over long-term reasoning almost every time.

For many clients, understanding this creates enormous relief.

What once felt like personal failure begins making physiological sense.

The Emotional Architecture of Financial Trauma

Fear sits near the center of many financial wounds: fear of loss, fear of judgment, fear of instability, or fear of returning to earlier experiences of helplessness and scarcity.

But fear rarely travels alone.

Shame frequently accompanies it, often emerging through quiet internal narratives such as: "I should have known better." "I'm bad with money." "Everyone else seems to understand this except me."

Shame has a profoundly silencing effect. It pushes financial concerns into secrecy, which unintentionally prevents the clarity, collaboration, and support that foster healing.

Over time, avoidance and shame begin reinforcing one another. The individual avoids looking at finances in order to escape anxiety. Avoidance increases uncertainty. Uncertainty amplifies fear. Fear deepens shame. The cycle continues, often operating largely outside conscious awareness.

Recognizing this loop often becomes a pivotal turning point in recovery. Once behavior is understood through a nervous system lens, self-condemnation frequently softens into something far more useful: informed compassion.

And compassion creates room for change.

A Clinical Illustration

Jill came to therapy describing persistent anxiety about money despite having a stable and objectively secure career. She checked her accounts repeatedly throughout the day, yet the behavior brought little relief. Even relatively minor unexpected expenses triggered disproportionate panic.

As we gradually explored her history, an important memory surfaced. During adolescence, Jill had witnessed her parents lose their home during a sudden financial collapse. Although her adult life looked very different externally, her nervous system had never fully updated its internal map of safety.

In many ways, her body was still living inside that earlier environment of unpredictability.

Importantly, healing did not begin with spreadsheets, budgeting systems, or financial strategy. It began by helping her nervous system experience present-day safety physiologically. We focused first on grounding, breath work, regulation practices, and gradual exposure to financial tasks while remaining within tolerable activation.

Only after her nervous system became less dominated by threat did practical financial planning begin feeling accessible and effective.

Months later, Jill described the shift in simple but powerful language:

"For the first time, I'm making choices from calm instead of fear."

That sentence captures the heart of Stage Three.

Expansion Into Agency

Stage Three healing is not about eliminating all financial fear. Life will always contain uncertainty. Markets fluctuate. Circumstances change. Unexpected loss remains part of the human experience.

Expansion instead reflects the nervous system's growing ability to remain internally organized even in the presence of uncertainty.

As regulation deepens, new questions begin emerging organically:

What does financial safety actually feel like in my body?

What values do I want my money to express?

What kind of future am I intentionally building?

These questions signal a profound developmental shift.

The nervous system is no longer operating entirely from contraction. It is beginning to tolerate expansion.

With increased regulation comes greater flexibility. Planning becomes more accessible. Creativity returns. Financial behavior begins aligning more closely with present-day values rather than earlier survival scripts. This is the gradual emergence of agency, and for many trauma survivors it initially feels both hopeful and unfamiliar.

Healing financial trauma requires both emotional and practical attention. Financial clarity matters. Planning matters. Structure matters. But sustainable financial change almost always begins with the nervous system itself.

A calmer system supports wiser decision-making. A more regulated body allows longer-term thinking. An integrated nervous system creates space for both caution and possibility simultaneously.

The goal is not financial perfection, nor is it the elimination of all uncertainty. The deeper goal is developing a fundamentally different relationship with money — one grounded in clarity, self-compassion, flexibility, and increasing self-leadership.

Expansion, in this context, means reclaiming authorship over the financial story rather than remaining confined to earlier survival chapters.

The Emergence of Earned Security

As financial threat gradually loses some of its physiological intensity, many individuals begin noticing subtle but meaningful internal changes.

There may be a slightly longer pause before reacting to financial stress. Decisions that once triggered immediate urgency begin feeling more spacious. The body, which previously braced constantly for impact, slowly softens its grip on vigilance.

From a trauma-informed perspective, this widening of internal capacity reflects far more than emotional improvement. It represents meaningful nervous system reorganization. When the body experiences enough moments of predictability, regulation, and successful adaptation, the brain gradually updates its internal models of safety.

In attachment language, this is part of the architecture of earned security.

Importantly, earned security does not require perfect financial circumstances. It reflects the growing ability to remain internally organized even when uncertainty inevitably appears. The nervous system becomes less dependent upon rigid control, avoidance, or panic and more capable of flexible, values-aligned response.

This is where Stage Three begins maturing.

As financial threat loses some of its physiological charge, attention naturally starts shifting outward. Energy that was once consumed by monitoring, bracing, worrying, or survival forecasting becomes increasingly available for thoughtful planning, intentional decision-making, creativity, and future-oriented vision.

In many ways, survival bandwidth begins transforming into agency bandwidth.

For nervous systems long organized around protection, this transition may feel unfamiliar at first. Periods of forward movement often alternate with temporary returns to older contraction patterns. This oscillation is not failure. It is a normal part of integration and nervous system reorganization.

What matters most is the overall direction of movement.

And as the nervous system settles into increasing safety, a new question naturally begins emerging: Not simply, "How do I protect what I have?"

But more expansively, "How do I wisely build what comes next?"

Chapter 13 - What Is Health Anyway?

"Well-being is a state of integration—where the different parts of a system are linked in a flexible and harmonious way." — Daniel J. Siegel

As the nervous system begins experiencing greater safety — around money, relationships, identity, and life more broadly — many individuals notice a subtle but meaningful internal shift. The urgency that once drove nearly every decision begins softening. Reactions that previously felt immediate and automatic now include a small but important pause.

From a clinical perspective, this pause reflects far more than psychological insight. It represents increasing flexibility within the autonomic nervous system itself. The system is becoming less dominated by chronic threat reactivity and more capable of adaptive regulation.

Within the Relational Nervous System Integration Model™, this is where expansion begins stabilizing into integration.

Earlier stages of healing focused primarily on survival: establishing safety, regulating activation, repairing attachment wounds, integrating embodied memory, and restoring increasing coherence within identity and relationship. But as these capacities strengthen, another question naturally begins emerging beneath the work:

What does genuine health actually look like?

This question is deceptively simple.

Many people unconsciously define health as the absence of symptoms, conflict, anxiety, sadness, or struggle. But from a neurobiological perspective, health is not the elimination of activation. It is the nervous system's increasing capacity for flexibility, recovery, adaptation, and coordinated integration.

Over the years in clinical practice, I have observed two regulatory patterns emerging repeatedly across individuals whose nervous systems have been shaped by chronic threat or instability.

Sometimes the system moves toward rigidity. A person longs for certainty, structure, predictability, and control. They may search intensely for the perfect plan, the correct method, or a guaranteed pathway toward healing. Beneath this longing is an understandable nervous system strategy. When life has felt unpredictable, increased control often becomes associated with safety.

Yet healthy systems are rarely rigid.

From a developmental and neurobiological standpoint, integrated systems demonstrate flexibility, variability, and adaptive responsiveness. When healing becomes excessively rigid or perfectionistic, sympathetic activation and internal strain often increase rather than resolve.

At other times, the opposite pattern emerges. Emotional experience becomes fragmented, overwhelming, or difficult to organize coherently. Thoughts race. Affect shifts rapidly. Internal experience feels noisy or chaotic because multiple unintegrated emotional and physiological networks are activating simultaneously.

Over time, I have come to understand that these two movements — rigidity and chaos — are not personality defects.

They are regulatory adaptations.

And if you have been moving thoughtfully through this book, you may already recognize both patterns within yourself. There may have been seasons when control and predictability felt safer than uncertainty. At other times, your internal world may have felt emotionally noisy, fragmented, or difficult to organize.

Neither pattern represents personal failure.

Both reflect the nervous system's attempt to maintain functional stability under conditions of perceived threat.

The River of Integration

This is where the work of Daniel J. Siegel offers a particularly useful organizing metaphor.

Siegel describes mental health as a river. On one bank lies rigidity; on the other lies chaos. Health emerges not through clinging to either extreme, but through the capacity to move fluidly between them with increasing flexibility and coherence.

From the perspective of interpersonal neurobiology, integration involves both differentiation and linkage. Distinct systems retain their individuality while remaining connected and communicative with one another. Emotional systems, cognitive systems, bodily awareness, relational perception, and autonomic regulation all function most effectively when they are coordinated rather than isolated or competing.

This is true not only psychologically, but biologically.

Healthy nervous systems are not static. They are adaptive.

We all move toward one bank or the other at times. Some degree of predictability is not only normal, but deeply regulating. My wife and I, for example, often find ourselves at the same pizza restaurant on Friday evenings. That small rhythm creates familiarity, continuity, and a quiet sense of safety within the nervous system.

But healthy functioning also requires movement toward novelty, spontaneity, creativity, and expansion. Friendships evolve. Interests deepen. New experiences stretch the nervous system's capacity for flexibility and adaptation.

Sustainable wellbeing depends on the ability to tolerate both sameness and change without becoming destabilized by either.

Within this framework, harmony is not static calm. It is coordinated complexity. Health reflects the nervous system's ability to remain organized while adapting fluidly to changing internal and external conditions.

As you reflect on earlier chapters, many previously confusing experiences may begin organizing themselves differently within this model. Hypervigilance, emotional flooding, protective numbing, dissociation, shutdown, perfectionism, or avoidance are not isolated malfunctions. They are states in which the nervous system has been pulled disproportionately toward one bank in an effort to preserve survival.

Recovery, then, is not about eliminating activation altogether.

It is about restoring flexible flow.

What Do We Mean by "Mind"?

We use the word mind constantly, yet in trauma work it helps to define it more carefully.

Siegel describes the mind as "an embodied and relational, emergent, self-organizing process that regulates the flow of energy and information." Although the definition initially sounds complex, each part reflects important findings from attachment research, affective neuroscience, and developmental psychology.

The mind is **embodied** because neural processing cannot be separated from physiological state. Trauma responses emerge through respiratory changes, muscular tension, cardiovascular activation, vagal shifts, posture, and autonomic reflexes long before conscious narrative develops fully. The body is continuously participating in emotional processing whether we are consciously aware of it or not.

The mind is also **relational.** Decades of attachment research demonstrate that regulatory capacity develops within co-regulating relationships. Early caregiver attunement shapes stress reactivity thresholds, autonomic flexibility, and emotional regulation capacity throughout development. Even in adulthood, emotional states remain profoundly influenced by the nervous system's ongoing assessment of relational safety or threat.

Healing therefore continues occurring within relationship, including the increasingly attuned relationship individuals develop with themselves.

The mind is **emergent** because it arises through dynamic interaction among neural networks, bodily states, memory systems, emotional experience, cognition, and relational input. No single structure "is" the mind. Rather, the mind reflects coordinated communication across systems, much like music emerging from an orchestra rather than from any single instrument alone.

Finally, the mind is **self-organizing**. It continuously monitors internal and external conditions while adjusting in response to changing demands. Defensive responses such as fight, flight, freeze, collapse, withdrawal, or hypervigilance are not evidence of pathology in themselves. They are adaptive survival programs mediated through subcortical threat circuitry. Difficulties arise primarily when these systems become chronically overactivated or insufficiently resolved.

Even in ordinary moments, you can observe this regulatory intelligence at work: pausing before responding defensively, taking a breath to stabilize during stress, or stepping back when stimulation exceeds capacity.

These are signs of an actively functioning regulatory system.

The Flow of Energy and Information

Another clinically useful way to understand the mind is to view it as the manager of how experience moves through the organism.

In neurobiological terms, energy refers to electrochemical signaling across neural pathways, autonomic systems, and bodily processes. Information refers to the meaning carried within those signals: emotions, memories, perceptions, somatic sensations, beliefs, relational cues, and cognitive interpretation.

An integrated system does not suppress emotional intensity. Rather, it allows activation to move through flexibly without becoming rigidly trapped in chronic hyperarousal or hypoarousal states.

Clinically, this flexibility supports the capacity to remain present during relational stress, shift adaptively between emotional states, maintain reflective functioning under pressure, and access empathy without losing discernment or boundaries.

Many of the practices explored throughout this book — grounding, orienting, breath regulation, somatic awareness, cognitive clarification, relational repair, and paced response — function by improving the efficiency and flexibility of this energy-and-information flow.

You have not simply been acquiring coping tools.

You have been strengthening the neural architecture of integration itself.

Moving Toward Health

One of the most reliable indicators of healing is that it often feels less dramatic than people expect.

Rather than arriving through a single breakthrough moment, integration more commonly appears through subtle but meaningful shifts in baseline functioning. Individuals notice activation earlier. They recover regulatory balance more quickly. They feel less compelled toward defensive overexplanation or emotional shutdown. Pause capacity increases under stress.

Although these changes are easy to overlook, they reflect meaningful improvements in autonomic flexibility and prefrontal-limbic coordination.

This represents an important developmental threshold within the Relational Nervous System Integration Model™. Earlier stages focused on understanding survival adaptations and restoring safety within the body, relationships, identity, and nervous system. From this point forward, the emphasis increasingly shifts from acquiring insight to embodying integration — living from a nervous system capable of sustaining both steadiness and openness without chronic destabilization.

The goal is not perfection.

The goal is a system capable of adaptive movement toward steadiness without rigidity, toward openness without chaos, and toward a form of health characterized by resilient, flexible self-organization.

In the chapters ahead, we will continue exploring what allows this integration not only to emerge in isolated moments, but to stabilize across the ordinary rhythms and demands of everyday life.

Chapter 14 - Your Complex Inner World

"The curious paradox is that when I accept myself just as I am, then I can change." — Carl Rogers

In the previous chapter, we explored health not as the absence of activation, but as increasing integration within the nervous system — the growing capacity for flexibility, adaptability, and coordinated self-organization. We examined the movement between rigidity and chaos and introduced the idea that healing involves restoring flexible flow rather than eliminating emotional intensity altogether.

As this integration begins stabilizing, many people notice something both surprising and quietly relieving: their inner world becomes easier to observe.

Not necessarily quieter at first, but clearer.

Reactions that once felt confusing or overwhelming begin revealing recognizable patterns. Emotional shifts that previously seemed random start making more sense. What once felt like "losing control" often turns out to be something far more organized — different parts of the nervous system stepping forward at different moments, each attempting, in its own way, to help the individual navigate the world safely.

Within the Relational Nervous System Integration Model™, this marks another important developmental deepening. Earlier stages focused primarily on stabilization, attachment, embodiment, and identity integration. Now the work expands toward understanding the internal system itself: the multiple emotional states, survival responses, and protective adaptations that together make up the lived experience of being human.

From a clinical perspective, the increasing ability to observe these inner shifts reflects meaningful neurobiological change. Prefrontal regulatory systems are becoming more integrated with subcortical emotional and survival networks. Put more simply, the nervous system is becoming increasingly capable of noticing itself in real time without immediately becoming overwhelmed by what it notices.

This growing observational capacity creates space for something profoundly important: internal leadership.

The Mind as a System of Parts

Tammy, a teacher in her forties, once said to me during a session, "Sometimes I feel like there's a whole committee inside me — the confident professional, the scared little girl, the harsh critic. I didn't realize this was normal until I learned about parts work."

If something in her description feels familiar, you are in very good company.

Most people, when they begin observing their internal experience carefully, discover that the mind is not a single, steady voice. It is far more dynamic. Different emotional states, perspectives, impulses, and protective responses emerge depending on context, perceived safety, and nervous system activation.

Contemporary trauma models such as Internal Family Systems developed by Richard C. Schwartz, ego state therapy, and state-dependent memory research all converge on a similar observation: multiplicity within the mind is normal.

This does not mean something is wrong with you.

It means your nervous system is functioning in a deeply human way.

In fact, we speak this language intuitively all the time, often without recognizing its clinical significance. Someone says, "Part of me wants to go out tonight, but another part of me wants to stay home." Statements like these reflect an implicit awareness that different mind-body states emerge under different conditions.

From a neurobiological perspective, these shifts often involve rapid changes in autonomic tone, limbic activation, memory networks, and prefrontal modulation occurring together beneath conscious awareness.

You may notice this in your own life. Around trusted friends, you may feel spontaneous, grounded, and emotionally open. Then a supervisor asks about a missing report or a partner's tone suddenly changes, and something inside reorganizes almost instantly. Your breathing shifts. Muscles tighten subtly. Self-consciousness increases. Your internal dialogue changes.

The shift is not merely psychological. It is physiological.

Modern neuroscience increasingly supports what many people intuitively experience: the mind naturally organizes into distinct but interacting states depending on context and perceived safety.

The Orchestra Within

One useful way to visualize this internal system is to imagine an orchestra.

At different moments, different instruments come forward. Sometimes the strings carry the melody while the percussion softens into the background. At other times, another section becomes dominant. Importantly, the other instruments do not disappear. They remain present within the larger system, ready to re-enter when needed.

When integration is strong, the music flows with coordination and timing. Different emotional states communicate flexibly with one another. Regulatory systems remain adaptive. The nervous system can shift between vulnerability, strength, reflection, playfulness, protection, and connection without becoming trapped in any one state.

When integration is strained, however, the experience can feel more chaotic internally.

Certain parts may dominate so completely that flexibility narrows. At other times, multiple states may compete simultaneously, creating internal overwhelm, confusion, or emotional fragmentation.

Clinically, this often corresponds with reduced autonomic flexibility and increased sympathetic or dorsal vagal dominance. But subjectively, it usually feels far more personal:

"I don't understand why I reacted so strongly."

"Part of me knew I was safe, but another part panicked."

"I felt like I became someone else."

As individuals begin recognizing these internal shifts with greater clarity, shame often starts softening. What once appeared irrational begins making nervous system sense.

Protective Parts and Survival Intelligence

Many of these internal states formed originally as intelligent survival adaptations.

An anxious part may have developed to anticipate danger before it arrived.

A perfectionistic part may have emerged to reduce criticism or rejection.

A withdrawn part may have learned that emotional invisibility increased safety.

A harsh inner critic may paradoxically believe that constant self-monitoring prevents humiliation or failure.

From the perspective of the nervous system, these parts are not enemies.

They are protective strategies shaped through earlier experience.

Tammy eventually recognized that her anxious, hypervigilant part developed during repeated experiences with a highly punitive teacher in childhood. Vigilance helped her anticipate criticism and avoid humiliation. Her nervous system learned efficiently.

Years later, similar authority dynamics automatically reactivated those same survival patterns through state-dependent memory networks. The response was not irrational. It was learned, encoded, and repeatedly reinforced.

Understanding this changes the tone of healing dramatically.

Instead of approaching the self with frustration or force, individuals begin approaching their inner world with curiosity, compassion, and increasing coherence.

Integration, Not Elimination

This is one of the most important principles within parts work and within the Relational Nervous System Integration Model™ more broadly: healing is not about eliminating parts of the self.

It is about increasing integration and coordination within the system.

Earlier in this book, we described trauma as experience that never fully found its proper place within the nervous system — information stored but insufficiently integrated. From this perspective, healing involves helping protective responses update their understanding of present reality rather than forcing them into silence.

The memory may remain, much like an instrument remaining part of the orchestra. What changes is the intensity of activation, the speed of triggering, and the quality of regulation guiding the overall system.

Many people can recall moments when emotion seemed to ambush them: a tone of voice, a facial expression, or a subtle relational cue suddenly triggering a reaction that felt disproportionate to the present moment.

In neurobiological terms, previously encoded survival networks activated rapidly and automatically.

What we are cultivating now is something fundamentally different.

Not the removal of protective parts, but the emergence of internal leadership capable of relating to those parts without becoming consumed by them.

The Emergence of Internal Leadership

Central to Richard C. Schwartz's Internal Family Systems model is the concept of the Self—a calm, compassionate, grounded organizing presence capable of relating to different emotional states without becoming overwhelmed by them.

Many clinicians observe that as this self-leadership strengthens, clients demonstrate greater affect tolerance, improved reflective capacity, and increasing autonomic regulation.

Sometimes I describe this process to clients as the difference between a committee without leadership and one guided by a skilled chairperson. The voices do not disappear. But coordination becomes increasingly possible.

Importantly, the very ability to notice these internal dynamics already reflects emerging metacognitive capacity. Something within you is observing the system rather than being entirely fused with it.

And that observing presence is where internal authority begins taking root.

Within the Relational Nervous System Integration Model™, this represents another important movement in Stage Three expansion. Earlier stages focused on reducing overwhelm and increasing stabilization. Now the nervous system is developing the capacity not only to regulate experience, but to organize experience consciously and compassionately from a more integrated center.

Anchoring in the Adult Self

One of the most powerful movements in trauma recovery involves repeatedly orienting toward the present-day adult self — the version of you that now possesses resources, perspective, support, and capacities that were unavailable earlier in life.

This process is not forced. It strengthens gradually through repeated orientation.

Sometimes the work appears deceptively simple: noticing objects in the room your younger self would never have known, feeling the support of the chair beneath your body, recognizing your current age, recalling challenges you have survived, or remembering relationships and capacities now available to you.

These are not psychological tricks.

They are nervous system updates.

They communicate a profoundly important orienting signal: I am here now.

James, a client working through significant childhood trauma, developed a quiet morning ritual designed to strengthen this adult-self orientation. Before beginning his day, he would pause to feel his feet on the floor, name his present age aloud, and remind himself of the supports and capacities available to him now.

Nothing dramatic occurred in these moments.

Yet over time, meaningful changes emerged. He reported fewer automatic threat reactions, faster recovery after stress, and a growing sense that he was responding from steadiness rather than survival urgency.

Without consciously trying to, he was strengthening internal leadership and increasing regulatory flexibility.

Working With Younger Parts

As fear, shame, grief, or vulnerability surfaces — and at times it inevitably will — the goal is not suppression.

Instead, the practice becomes one of gentle dual awareness.

An individual might notice: "There is a frightened younger part of me here right now." And simultaneously: "I am also here — the adult who is observing this experience."

From this more integrated stance, reassurance becomes possible. The adult self can begin relating to activated parts with steadiness rather than fear:

"We are safe enough right now."

"I can handle this moment."

"This feeling makes sense."

Repeated consistently over time, this internal dialogue gradually builds trust across the nervous system. Protective parts no longer need to escalate with the same intensity because the system increasingly experiences internal coordination and leadership.

Contemporary trauma therapy increasingly emphasizes respectful inner communication rather than forceful control. Curiosity tends to foster integration far more effectively than internal warfare.

Many people find gentle reflective practices helpful during this stage of healing. Questions such as "What does this part of me need right now?" or "What is this reaction trying to protect?" often create more integration than attempts to suppress emotion immediately.

In many cases, attuned listening itself becomes healing.

From Awareness to Real-Time Integration

As internal leadership strengthens, an important developmental shift begins occurring within the Relational Nervous System Integration Model™. Awareness gradually moves from retrospective understanding into real-time application.

Individuals begin recognizing activation while it is happening rather than only afterward.

They notice tightening in the chest before panic fully escalates. They recognize the voice of the inner critic before becoming completely fused with shame. They sense withdrawal impulses emerging before disappearing emotionally from relationships.

This is where integration becomes increasingly embodied and practical.

The goal is not perfect internal harmony. Human nervous systems remain dynamic and complex. The goal is growing capacity — the ability to remain increasingly present, organized, and compassionate while navigating the inevitable movements of the inner world.

One client captured this shift beautifully after months of work: “I’m learning to be the loving adult I always needed.”

Another said: “I’m not trying to fix myself anymore. I’m learning to work with my system’s wisdom.”

Both statements reflect the same profound movement. Integration is taking hold.

And as this internal coordination strengthens, an important question naturally begins emerging:

How do we work with these nervous system shifts in real time when life becomes activating?

In the next chapter, we will move from understanding the internal system toward developing practical, moment-by-moment strategies for working with activation as it unfolds. We will begin exploring how awareness, regulation, and internal leadership come together not only in reflection, but in the lived moments that matter most.

Chapter 15 - How Bodies Release Learned Patterns

"Trauma is not what happens to us, but what we hold inside." — Peter Levine

In the previous chapter, we explored the complex inner world of the nervous system — the shifting emotional states, protective parts, and internal patterns that emerge depending on context, memory, and perceived safety. As internal leadership strengthens, many individuals begin recognizing their reactions with increasing clarity rather than becoming immediately overwhelmed by them.

At a certain point, however, a very practical question naturally begins to emerge: What do I actually do in the moment when my body becomes activated?

Understanding the nervous system intellectually is an important milestone. Learning how to work with it in real time is where integration begins stabilizing into lived experience.

Within the Relational Nervous System Integration Model™, this chapter marks another important developmental movement in Stage Three: Expansion. Earlier phases focused on stabilization, attachment, embodiment, identity, and internal awareness. Now the emphasis shifts toward active participation in nervous system repatterning itself — learning how moment-by-moment experiences gradually reshape physiology, regulation, and emotional flexibility over time.

To enter this conversation, let me begin with something ordinary.

Every few years I find myself back on a golf course for the first game of the season. Standing at the first tee, I take my time. I rehearse the swing carefully. I visualize the ball sailing cleanly down the fairway. And then, despite all that thoughtful intention, the ball traces a beautiful arc directly into the woods.

It is not bad luck, nor is it a failure of visualization. It is simply a motor pattern my body has practiced enough times that it now unfolds automatically. The body remembers what it has rehearsed.

That small moment on the golf course offers a useful doorway into something far more consequential: the way the nervous system learns patterns — and the encouraging reality that learned patterns can gradually be reshaped through new experience.

Modern neuroscience and trauma research consistently point toward something both humbling and hopeful. Much of what we experience as "reaction" is not primarily a conscious choice. It is the nervous system drawing upon previously encoded survival pathways designed to preserve safety.

From this perspective, trauma responses are not signs of weakness or irrationality. They are highly efficient adaptations shaped through lived experience.

By this point in your journey through the book, you may already notice a subtle shift occurring in your internal dialogue. Instead of asking, "Why do I react this way?" you may increasingly find yourself asking, "What did my body learn that made this response necessary?"

That question carries a profoundly different emotional tone. Curiosity begins replacing self-condemnation. Understanding softens shame. And this is often where meaningful nervous system change begins.

The body continuously learns through repetition. Every time an experience becomes paired with fear, helplessness, urgency, criticism, abandonment, or danger, neural pathways strengthen around those associations. Over time, the nervous system becomes increasingly efficient at predicting and preparing for similar situations in the future.

This learning process is not inherently negative. It is survival intelligence. The encouraging reality, however, is that the nervous system can also learn new patterns through repeated experiences of regulation, safety, recovery, and embodied completion.

Consider a simple and familiar moment. You are reading a bedtime story to your child. Your breathing is relatively steady. Your body feels reasonably calm. Attention is focused and connected.

Then your phone rings.

A stressful message appears on the screen. Within seconds, your physiology shifts. Heart rate increases. Breath shortens. Muscles tighten subtly. Attention narrows toward potential threat.

Nothing is wrong with you in that moment. Your nervous system has simply shifted into a different state of organization.

Now imagine that after the call ends, you pause intentionally before moving forward. You take two slower breaths. You remind yourself quietly, "There is nothing I need to solve right now." As your attention returns to your child, you notice your shoulders gradually softening again.

The body has not changed. The situation has not entirely changed. But a different pathway is beginning to emerge — one that is increasingly intentional rather than purely automatic.

This distinction is extremely important within the Relational Nervous System Integration Model™. Healing does not mean preventing all state shifts. Healthy nervous systems are designed to move fluidly between activation and recovery depending on circumstance. Integration instead involves gradually increasing the capacity to participate consciously in the return to regulation.

Sue, a nurse I once worked with, described leaving every hospital shift feeling chronically depleted and tightly wound. As we explored her experience more carefully, she began noticing something subtle but important: between patients, her body never fully reset. Even during brief pauses, her nervous system was already bracing for the next demand.

Her physiology had learned continuous anticipatory activation.

Once she recognized the pattern, we introduced very small regulatory resets into her day. While washing her hands between patients, she practiced taking one slower breath. She noticed the temperature of the water. She felt the texture of the towel as she dried her hands. Occasionally she paused for just a few seconds to feel both feet on the floor before entering the next room.

None of these interventions were dramatic, nor did they eliminate the demands of her environment. But over time, something measurable shifted. She began carrying less accumulated tension home at the end of the day. Her recovery after stressful interactions improved. The nervous system was receiving more frequent signals of completion, pause, and regulation rather than remaining trapped in continuous mobilization.

This illustrates an important clinical principle: regulation capacity often develops through repeated small resets rather than dramatic emotional breakthroughs. The nervous system changes through repetition, and small experiences matter because the body encodes patterns cumulatively.

By now you have encountered the basic language of the autonomic nervous system: sympathetic activation supporting mobilization and parasympathetic pathways supporting restoration, connection, and recovery. Rather than holding these concepts abstractly, it becomes increasingly helpful to observe how these shifts already move through your daily life. You may begin noticing moments when your body mobilizes rapidly, moments when it softens naturally, and moments when it struggles to return fully to balance after stress.

From a trauma-informed perspective, health is not defined by remaining permanently calm. In fact, a nervous system incapable of mobilization would not be healthy at all. Health is better understood as regulatory flexibility — the capacity to move into activation when necessary and return from it without becoming chronically stuck.

Many individuals begin recognizing early markers of this flexibility long before they consider themselves "fully healed." They recover more quickly after difficult conversations. They notice tension earlier in its rise. They respond to themselves more gently during activation rather than escalating shame internally.

Although these shifts may appear small externally, neurobiologically they reflect meaningful nervous system learning already underway.

Daniel J. Siegel uses the term mindsight to describe the capacity to observe inner experience with steadiness and clarity. Neurobiologically, this capacity is associated with increasing integration between prefrontal regulatory regions and limbic emotional systems.

In practical terms, mindsight allows individuals to notice what is happening inside them without becoming entirely swept away by it.

At this stage of the Relational Nervous System Integration Model™, mindful awareness becomes less about performing exercises perfectly and more about cultivating a different internal posture toward experience itself. You notice. You stay curious. You allow internal states to emerge without immediately attempting to suppress, judge, or fix them.

Even brief moments of awareness begin strengthening internal leadership.

You may notice your breathing without changing it. You may observe where your body feels settled and where it feels activated. You may become aware of tightening in the jaw, constriction in the chest, or subtle shifts in posture as emotional states arise. This kind of noticing is not passive. It is regulation through awareness.

And over time, awareness itself becomes increasingly organizing for the nervous system.

Several body-oriented trauma therapies, including Sensorimotor Psychotherapy developed by Pat Ogden and Somatic Experiencing developed by Peter A. Levine, propose that trauma often involves protective responses that were mobilized but never fully completed. The body prepared to defend, flee, protest, protect, or escape — but the sequence became interrupted.

From this perspective, healing is often less about endlessly retelling the story and more about helping the nervous system experience completion and resolution gradually, within tolerable levels of activation.

Sometimes this occurs through subtle movement. Sometimes through increased awareness of sensation. Sometimes through repeated experiences of safety while remaining emotionally present. Sometimes through the simple recognition that the body is no longer trapped in the original danger.

Importantly, the goal is not emotional catharsis for its own sake. The goal is integration.

This reframing can feel profoundly relieving for many trauma survivors. The body is no longer viewed as the problem to overcome. Instead, it becomes understood as the part of the self that has been working — often tirelessly — to preserve survival.

As new experiences accumulate — moments of safety, pauses of awareness, successful recovery after activation, and small acts of self-regulation — the nervous system gradually updates its predictions about the world. Earlier threat expectations begin loosening as new physiological data repeatedly arrives.

This process rarely feels dramatic in real time. More often, it unfolds quietly.

You may simply notice one day that something which once overwhelmed you now feels more manageable. A difficult conversation no longer ruins the entire day. A moment of criticism no longer spirals immediately into shame. Recovery comes more quickly. Breathing returns more easily.

Not because you forced yourself to change, but because your system has been learning another way to respond.

Within the Relational Nervous System Integration Model™, this is where expansion becomes increasingly embodied. Regulation is no longer experienced merely as something practiced occasionally. It begins becoming integrated into the nervous system's baseline organization.

And as this capacity strengthens, another important developmental threshold begins to emerge. If the nervous system can learn new patterns, if internal leadership can strengthen, and if activation can increasingly be met with steadiness rather than fear, then an important question naturally follows:

How do we intentionally build environments, relationships, and rhythms of life that help this regulation stabilize over time?

In the next chapter, we will widen the lens outward again, exploring the external conditions that support long-term nervous system healing and integration. Because while inner work is essential, sustainable recovery is rarely an entirely solitary process. The nervous system was shaped in relationship, and it continues to heal there.

Chapter 16 - The Window of Tolerance

"Between stimulus and response there is a space. In that space is our power to choose our response." —Viktor E. Frankl

In the previous chapter, we explored how the nervous system gradually relearns safety through repeated experiences of awareness, regulation, and embodied completion. We examined how healing often unfolds not through dramatic breakthroughs, but through the steady repatterning of physiological responses over time. As those capacities begin strengthening, many individuals notice an important shift occurring in daily life: they become increasingly able to recognize activation while it is happening rather than only afterward.

And with that awareness comes an important question: How do I recognize, in real time, when my nervous system is beginning to move toward overwhelm — and how do I help it return?

This is where the concept of the window of tolerance becomes especially useful within the Relational Nervous System Integration Model™. Earlier stages focused on stabilization, attachment, identity, embodiment, and the development of internal leadership. This chapter builds directly upon those foundations by helping individuals understand the dynamic range within which the nervous system can remain flexible, emotionally connected, and physiologically regulated.

The concept was originally developed by Daniel J. Siegel to describe the zone in which the nervous system can tolerate emotional intensity without shifting into states of overwhelm or shutdown. When functioning within this range, individuals are generally able to think clearly, remain emotionally connected, reflect before reacting, and stay grounded in present reality even during stress.

Importantly, the window of tolerance is not a fixed emotional state of permanent calm. It is better understood as a flexible bandwidth of nervous system capacity.

A useful comparison is the thermostat inside a home. A healthy thermostat does not hold the temperature at one exact number all day long. Instead, it allows for natural fluctuations while helping the system remain within a functional and livable range. Your nervous system has been attempting something similar throughout your life. Not always perfectly. Not always smoothly. But persistently.

When activation remains within your window of tolerance, stress may still be present, but the nervous system retains flexibility. You can adapt, reflect, problem-solve, and remain connected to yourself and others. When activation moves beyond that range, however, the system begins shifting into protective physiology.

For many individuals living with chronic stress or unresolved trauma, this is not merely theoretical language. It describes daily experience.

Candace once described an afternoon at the grocery store where rising prices left her feeling frustrated and tense. Yet she remained able to compare options, adjust her plan, and stay emotionally present. Her nervous system was activated, but still regulated.

On another morning, however, she was rushing to get her son ready for school when he spilled milk across his shirt moments before they needed to leave. Almost instantly, her body surged into activation. Her voice became sharp. Her breathing tightened. The intensity of her reaction startled even her.

Later, shame followed quickly behind.

Viewed through the lens of the window of tolerance, however, the situation becomes far more understandable. In that moment, the accumulated stress within Candace's nervous system exceeded her available regulatory capacity. Her body moved beyond its upper threshold and into protective survival activation.

This reframing becomes one of the most compassionate shifts in trauma-informed work. Instead of asking, "What is wrong with me?" individuals begin asking, "Where was my nervous system at that moment?"

That question changes the emotional tone of healing entirely. It introduces both clarity and compassion.

When the nervous system moves outside its optimal regulatory range, it generally shifts in one of two broad directions, both deeply rooted in autonomic survival physiology.

The first is hyperarousal, a state associated primarily with sympathetic activation. In hyperarousal, the body mobilizes for protection. Thoughts accelerate. Anxiety intensifies. Muscles tighten. Irritability rises. Attention narrows toward potential danger. Fight, flight, or defensive freezing responses become increasingly accessible.

In genuinely threatening situations, this response is highly adaptive. The body is designed to mobilize rapidly when danger appears. But when trauma has sensitized the nervous system, the alarm may activate in response to situations that are stressful but not objectively dangerous: a sharp tone of voice, relational tension, perceived criticism, time pressure, or unexpected change.

The response is not consciously chosen. It is automatically retrieved from previously encoded survival pathways.

On the opposite end lies hypoarousal, often associated with dorsal vagal shutdown. Rather than mobilizing, the nervous system conserves energy through disengagement and collapse. Individuals may experience emotional numbness, heaviness, disconnection, exhaustion, brain fog, or a sense of watching life from a distance.

Importantly, this state is not laziness or lack of motivation. It is a protective conservation strategy deployed when the nervous system determines that activation has become too overwhelming to manage effectively.

One of trauma's most discouraging effects is that it frequently narrows the window of tolerance itself. When the nervous system spends prolonged periods in survival physiology, it often becomes more sensitive to perceived threat and slower to recover once activated.

Clinically, this may appear as activating more quickly, feeling overwhelmed by relatively minor stressors, taking longer to return to baseline, or oscillating repeatedly between anxiety and shutdown.

If this has been your experience, it is important to state this clearly and compassionately: you did not choose this sensitivity. Your nervous system learned it through adaptation. And what has been learned can, with sufficient safety and repetition, gradually be reshaped.

This understanding points toward an essential clarification within the Relational Nervous System Integration Model™. The goal of healing is not to remain permanently inside the window of tolerance. Healthy nervous systems naturally move through cycles of activation and recovery in response to life's demands.

The true goal is expanded capacity and greater flexibility.

As healing progresses, individuals often begin noticing subtle but meaningful changes. They recognize dysregulation earlier. Recovery becomes faster. The body requires less intensity to regain steadiness. Emotional connection remains more accessible even under stress.

At first, these changes may feel almost disappointingly subtle. Yet this is very often how authentic nervous system healing unfolds — gradually, quietly, and cumulatively.

Part of this process involves developing what we might call nervous system literacy: learning to recognize what different forms of activation require in order to return toward regulation.

When the nervous system is in hyperarousal — too much, too fast — it often benefits from cues of settling and containment. Slow breathing with extended exhalation can help regulate autonomic activation. Grounding through sensory awareness may restore present-time orientation. Rhythmic movement such as walking can discharge excess sympathetic energy. Visually orienting to the environment reminds the nervous system that the present moment differs from earlier threat states.

When the system shifts toward hypoarousal — too little, too late — different forms of support are often needed. Gentle movement, cool water on the face or hands, music with steady rhythm, exposure to light, or safe relational contact may help reintroduce engagement and mobilization gradually.

Notice what is happening here. You are not forcing yourself to "be better."

You are learning the language of your nervous system. This is not self-control in the rigid sense.

It is self-leadership.

One of the most stabilizing practices individuals can develop during this stage of healing is what I often call a personal regulation map: an increasingly clear understanding of how their own nervous system functions.

People begin noticing what it feels like to remain inside their window of tolerance. They recognize the stressors that tend pushing them toward the edges. They learn which practices reliably help them return.

Importantly, this learning does not occur through perfection. The nervous system learns primarily through repeated noticing.

And one often-overlooked principle matters enormously here: regulation skills strengthen most effectively when practiced during relatively calm moments rather than only during crisis. We strengthen the return pathway when the nervous system is regulated enough to encode the experience successfully.

This is one reason stabilization remains foundational within the Relational Nervous System Integration Model™. Just as surgeons stabilize the body before attempting deeper repair, the nervous system requires sufficient physiological steadiness before deeper emotional integration can occur safely.

The window of tolerance therefore serves a much larger purpose than simply helping individuals "cope" with stress. It creates the internal conditions necessary for deeper healing, reflection, emotional processing, and integration to unfold without overwhelming the system.

And as stabilization becomes more reliable, many people begin noticing another important shift.

Once the nervous system can remain increasingly present during activation, deeper emotional material often begins surfacing naturally. Memories, grief, fear, shame, vulnerability, and unfinished emotional experiences may emerge into awareness with greater clarity than before.

This raises an important developmental question: How do we work safely and effectively with the deeper emotional layers that begin emerging once regulation becomes more reliable?

That is where we turn next. Because expanding the window of tolerance is not the final destination of healing.

It is what makes deeper integration possible.

Chapter 17 - Building Your Regulation Skills

"The body has a language. Learning to listen to it is part of healing." — Peter A. Levine

In the previous chapter, we explored the concept of the window of tolerance and examined how the nervous system moves dynamically between regulation, hyperarousal, and shutdown. We saw that healing does not mean remaining permanently calm, but rather developing greater flexibility, increased recovery capacity, and a wider range within which the nervous system can remain connected and adaptive.

As that understanding deepens, many people naturally begin asking a practical question: How do I actually support my nervous system when it begins drifting toward overwhelm or disconnection?

This is where regulation skills become especially important within the Relational Nervous System Integration Model™. Earlier stages of the model focused on stabilization, attachment, embodiment, identity, and the development of internal awareness. In the previous chapter, we explored how to recognize nervous system states more clearly in real time. Now we move into a more active phase of participation: developing practical ways to work collaboratively with the body as activation unfolds.

Importantly, the practices in this chapter are not designed to "fix" you. They are not evidence that your nervous system is broken, nor are they proof that you are somehow failing at healing.

Quite the opposite.

Each of these tools is better understood as a way of partnering respectfully with a nervous system that has been working — often tirelessly — to protect you. As your window of tolerance expands and your capacity for noticing increases, these practices simply provide additional ways to participate consciously in your own regulation.

By this point in the journey, you may already be recognizing some of the early signs that your system is drifting toward one edge or the other. Perhaps you notice tightening in your chest before anxiety fully escalates, or a subtle heaviness before emotional shutdown begins. This chapter offers possibilities for responding to those moments with greater skill, flexibility, and self-leadership.

No two nervous systems are identical. What feels deeply grounding to one person may feel insufficient or even uncomfortable to another. The goal is not mastery of every technique. The goal is growing familiarity with what helps your own system move back toward balance.

I will touch briefly on some of the science behind these approaches, but more importantly, I want you to experience them as respectful conversations with your body rather than rigid protocols to perform perfectly.

At times, the nervous system shifts into heightened activation: anxiety, agitation, racing thoughts, emotional flooding, irritability, or muscular tension. From an autonomic perspective, sympathetic mobilization has moved beyond what currently feels manageable.

When this happens, the task is not to forcibly shut the system down. Attempting to overpower activation often increases internal struggle. Instead, we offer the body reliable cues of safety and containment that gradually allow defensive mobilization to soften.

One of the most well-supported pathways for calming physiological arousal involves diaphragmatic breathing and the vagus nerve, the primary bidirectional communication pathway between body and brain. Research associated with Stephen Porges demonstrates that significantly more sensory information travels upward from the body to the brain than the reverse. This helps explain why body-based interventions often regulate the nervous system more effectively than purely cognitive efforts.

Slow diaphragmatic breathing increases parasympathetic tone and signals that the body is safe enough to reduce defensive activation. Some people find it helpful to imagine a balloon resting gently within the abdomen. As they inhale, the balloon expands softly. As they exhale, it settles and softens.

Even two or three minutes of slower breathing can begin creating measurable shifts: reduced muscular tension, clearer thinking, softer emotional intensity, and a subtle increase in internal spaciousness.

Other forms of regulation work primarily through sensory grounding. When emotional intensity rises, attention often collapses inward toward catastrophic thinking, fear loops, or emotionally charged imagery. Sensory grounding gently redirects awareness back toward present-time sensory reality.

In trauma therapy, this process is sometimes referred to as orienting, a concept emphasized within Sensorimotor Psychotherapy developed by Pat Ogden. The nervous system is continuously scanning the environment for cues of safety or danger. Orienting helps update that assessment in real time.

This is not distraction. It is reorientation.

Someone might slowly sip warm tea and notice its temperature and texture. Another person may wrap themselves in a weighted blanket and feel the steady pressure against the body. Others visually scan the room and name ordinary objects around them. These simple sensory experiences help anchor the nervous system in present reality rather than in remembered threat.

In effect, the body receives a new message: I am here now. This moment is different from the past.

Progressive muscle relaxation works through a slightly different mechanism. Originally developed by physician Edmund Jacobson, the practice teaches the nervous system to recognize relaxation through contrast. By intentionally tensing and then releasing different muscle groups, individuals often become aware of how much baseline tension they have been carrying outside conscious awareness.

The body gradually learns the difference between bracing and softening.

Over time, this increases proprioceptive awareness — the nervous system's ability to sense internal muscular and bodily states — while also supporting parasympathetic settling.

At other times, however, the nervous system shifts in the opposite direction. Instead of anxiety or hyperactivation, individuals may experience numbness, heaviness, fogginess, exhaustion, or emotional disconnection. Within polyvagal theory, this often reflects increasing dominance of dorsal vagal shutdown physiology.

In these moments, the goal is not calming. The goal is gentle re-engagement.

The nervous system often responds particularly well to rhythmic movement because rhythm and predictability communicate safety at a physiological level. Slow walking, rocking, swaying, stretching, or gentle movement to music can help restore engagement without overwhelming the system further.

Importantly, this is not movement for performance or fitness. It is movement for reconnection.

Certain forms of sensory input may also help bring the nervous system gradually back online. Cool water on the face or hands, invigorating scents such as peppermint or citrus, textured objects, steady rhythmic music, or walking barefoot across varied surfaces may all provide activating sensory information that gently increases engagement.

The intention here is modest mobilization — enough to help the system re-enter connection and presence without overshooting into hyperarousal.

As individuals begin experimenting with these practices, something subtle but important often begins shifting internally. Regulation becomes less about performing the "correct" technique and more about recognizing what the nervous system needs in the moment. People begin developing fluency in their own physiology.

Over time, this process often becomes increasingly intuitive. Sometimes the body needs settling. Sometimes it needs activation. Sometimes it simply needs a brief pause, slower breathing, or a moment of orientation before continuing forward.

This is the early emergence of a more collaborative internal relationship.

And within the Relational Nervous System Integration Model™, that collaboration represents meaningful progress. Earlier stages focused heavily on surviving activation. Now the nervous system is gradually learning flexibility, responsiveness, and increasing trust in its own ability to return.

Kindness matters deeply during this stage of healing. If a particular practice feels overwhelming or appears to move your system further outside the window of tolerance, that is not failure. It is useful information. The nervous system communicates continuously, and part of regulation work involves learning how to listen rather than force.

Sometimes the most regulating response is simply pausing, orienting visually to the room, feeling the support beneath your feet, and allowing the body a few moments of settling before doing anything else.

Regulation is not something you impose harshly upon yourself. It is something you invite, support, and strengthen gradually through repetition.

And as this capacity deepens, many individuals begin noticing that regulation tools become less about managing isolated moments of stress and more about supporting an entirely different relationship with their body, emotions, and inner world.

At a certain point, another important developmental shift begins occurring.

The nervous system becomes stable enough that deeper emotional material can begin surfacing more clearly. Old grief, unresolved fear, attachment pain, shame, vulnerability, and emotionally charged memories often emerge with greater accessibility once the system no longer spends all of its energy simply trying to survive moment-to-moment activation.

This raises an important next question: How do we work safely with deeper emotional material once sufficient regulation and stability have been established?

That is where we now turn.

Because the regulation skills you are building here are not the end of the work.

They are what make the next layer of integration possible.

Part III - Healing Through Connection

Within the Relational Nervous System Integration Model™, healing gradually moves from stabilization within the self toward increasing integration through relationship. As nervous system regulation strengthens, the capacity for safe connection begins expanding as well.

Human nervous systems do not regulate in isolation.

From our earliest moments in life, emotional stability develops through relationship — through the subtle exchange of safety, attunement, and shared presence. Trauma can disrupt these relational pathways, leaving the system feeling alone even in the presence of others.

In this section, we explore the biology of connection: neural resonance, mirror neurons, co-regulation, and the ways nervous systems continuously influence one another.

Understanding these relational dynamics opens the door to a powerful realization: healing does not happen only within the individual mind. It unfolds in the space between people, where safety and connection gradually reshape the nervous system's expectations of the world.

Chapter 18 - Building Neural Resonance

"The nervous system of one person helps regulate the nervous system of another." — Stephen Porges

In the previous chapter, we focused on the practical tools that help regulate the nervous system from within — breathing, grounding, movement, sensory awareness, and gentle activation. Those practices are foundational because they strengthen self-awareness and increase the nervous system's capacity for flexibility and internal leadership.

But as many people eventually discover, regulation is not solely an individual process.

Human nervous systems were never designed to function entirely alone.

As internal stability begins strengthening, another important layer of healing often starts to emerge within the Relational Nervous System Integration Model™: the experience of regulation in relationship. Earlier chapters explored how attachment shapes the nervous system and how trauma disrupts safety, embodiment, and identity. More recently, we have focused on strengthening the individual's ability to recognize and work with activation directly. Now the lens widens again toward something profoundly relational: the ways nervous systems continuously influence one another through connection, attunement, and presence.

This is where we encounter the remarkable phenomenon known as *co-regulation*, or what we might more broadly describe as neural resonance.

A client named Lisa once described a moment during therapy that illustrates this process beautifully. She had been recounting painful memories of bullying during her teenage years. As she spoke, I noticed her becoming increasingly flooded. Her breathing quickened, her posture subtly collapsed inward, and her attention narrowed more deeply into the emotional memory.

Gently, I invited her to pause and "come back into the office" with me. I asked her to look at my face for a few seconds and simply notice that we were here, in the present moment, together.

Later in the session, Lisa reflected on what she had experienced.

"I could feel myself getting overwhelmed thinking about what those girls were saying," she explained. "My chest was tight, and I felt myself shrinking. But when you asked me to look at you, my heart actually started slowing down. It felt like my system was borrowing your calm."

Her description captures something interpersonal neurobiology has increasingly documented over the past several decades: under conditions of perceived safety, one regulated nervous system can help stabilize another.

To understand how this works, it helps to return briefly to early development.

From the earliest months of life, human regulation is profoundly relational. The caregiver–infant relationship functions through what developmental researchers describe as co-regulation, a dynamic process in which both nervous systems continuously influence and respond to one another. In healthy environments, caregivers and infants gradually fall into natural synchrony. Facial expressions mirror. Vocal tones soften and adjust. Breathing rhythms coordinate. Heart rate patterns begin aligning.

Most of this occurs automatically and outside conscious awareness.

When these experiences unfold consistently enough, the child's nervous system gradually internalizes the experience of being soothed, emotionally organized, and physiologically settled in the presence of another person. This becomes part of the early architecture of secure attachment.

And importantly — this is one of the hopeful realities of nervous system healing — the capacity for resonance remains available throughout the lifespan.

Although the parent–child relationship is where co-regulation develops most rapidly, adult nervous systems continue demonstrating measurable synchronization during safe, attuned interaction. Research associated with Daniel J. Siegel, Allan Schore, and Stephen Porges increasingly suggests that under supportive conditions, adults may experience subtle alignment of breathing rhythms, shifts in heart rate variability, reduced sympathetic activation, softening of facial musculature, and increased ventral vagal regulation during emotionally safe connection.

In ordinary language, this is often experienced very simply:

"I feel calmer when I'm with you."

"Something about this conversation settled me."

"I didn't realize how tense I was until I sat here."

Lisa later described the experience in the therapy room this way: "It's like my body finally had a template for peace."

That sentence captures something deeply important about neural resonance. The nervous system does not only calm itself through internal effort. It also learns through repeated exposure to regulated others.

Within the Relational Nervous System Integration Model™, this marks another important developmental shift. Earlier stages emphasized building internal stabilization because trauma often leaves individuals feeling physiologically isolated inside their own survival states. As healing progresses, however, the nervous system gradually becomes more capable of allowing safety to move across relational space.

Healing begins occurring not only within the individual, but between individuals.

Several years ago, I observed a compelling demonstration of this process during professional training with Gary Brothers, who refers to this phenomenon as Interpersonal Interoceptive Resonance.

Two volunteers sat facing each other. One participant first spent several moments settling inward — slowing the breath, sensing the body, and shifting attention away from analytical thinking toward embodied awareness. Once centered, the participant made soft eye contact with the second volunteer, who had been intentionally focusing on a particular emotional state. After several moments, the centered participant described what they sensed emotionally.

With surprising accuracy, they identified the general emotional tone.

Experiences like this should not be interpreted as mystical mind-reading. Rather, they illustrate how remarkably sensitive the nervous system becomes to subtle relational cues when sufficiently regulated and attentive. Facial musculature, breathing shifts, vocal tone, posture, microexpressions, pacing, and autonomic signals all communicate information continuously beneath conscious awareness.

Human beings are relationally perceptive organisms.

And trauma often disrupts that perception in complicated ways.

For some individuals, the nervous system becomes hypervigilant toward relational danger while simultaneously struggling to recognize safety. Others become emotionally disconnected from relational cues altogether because closeness itself has historically been associated with pain, unpredictability, or overwhelm.

This is why co-regulation work can initially feel both relieving and unfamiliar for trauma survivors. The nervous system may deeply long for connection while simultaneously remaining cautious of it.

As regulation and resonance strengthen over time, however, many individuals begin recognizing an important new possibility: I do not have to regulate entirely alone.

Repeated experiences of safe relational resonance gradually introduce new neural associations into the system. The body learns that closeness does not always predict danger. Emotional presence does not always end in rejection. Vulnerability can coexist with regulation rather than collapse.

Over time, this often supports greater emotional flexibility, improved recovery from stress, increased capacity for intimacy, and a stronger baseline sense of safety within relationships.

One client expressed this shift beautifully:

"I'm learning that safety isn't just about being alone. It's about finding the right rhythms with other people."

That insight reflects a profound developmental movement. Many trauma survivors unconsciously organize around extreme self-reliance because depending on others once felt dangerous or disappointing. While the capacity to be comfortably alone is healthy and important, rigid isolation may also function as a protective adaptation.

Learning to remain regulated in the presence of safe others builds something deeply stabilizing inside the nervous system.

Fortunately, this capacity can often be strengthened in very gentle ways. Sometimes healing connection begins not through intense emotional disclosure, but through simple shared presence. Sitting quietly beside someone trusted. Walking together without pressure. Sharing calm conversation. Noticing the body soften slightly during safe interaction.

Some individuals find it helpful to observe their nervous system before, during, and after emotionally meaningful interactions. Before the interaction, they may notice their internal state. During the interaction, they might observe subtle shifts in breathing, muscular tension, emotional tone, or bodily settling. Afterward, they may reflect briefly on what changed.

This is not about constant self-monitoring. It is about developing relational literacy.

As awareness deepens, many people begin noticing meaningful shifts in how their nervous systems organize in connection. Emotional flexibility increases. Self-regulation becomes more reliable. Reactivity softens within close relationships. Moments of relational safety become easier to recognize and sustain.

These are not merely pleasant emotional experiences. They reflect measurable changes in how the nervous system organizes itself in relationship to others.

And as co-regulation becomes increasingly familiar, another important layer of healing often begins surfacing more clearly.

Many people start noticing that old attachment patterns — patterns formed long before they possessed the skills and awareness they are now developing — begin emerging more visibly within relationships. Fears of abandonment, emotional withdrawal, hypervigilance, people-pleasing, conflict avoidance, or difficulty trusting may all become easier to recognize as the nervous system grows more regulated and self-aware.

This naturally raises an important next question: How do we work with attachment patterns that were formed long before we had the capacities we are building now?

That is where we now turn. Because regulation and resonance are powerful.

But their deepest impact often unfolds in the landscape of attachment itself.

Chapter 19 -Neurons of Connection

"The mind is created within relationships."
— Daniel J. Siegel

In the previous chapter, we explored the lived experience of co-regulation — the way one steady nervous system can help another begin to settle. We examined how human beings are biologically designed not only for self-regulation, but for shared regulation through relationship. As nervous systems become increasingly capable of recognizing safety, many individuals begin discovering something profoundly hopeful: calm, trust, and emotional steadiness can gradually be learned through repeated relational experience.

At this point in the Relational Nervous System Integration Model™, the framework continues widening beyond the isolated individual and into the biology of connection itself. Earlier chapters focused on stabilization, embodiment, identity, regulation, and the development of internal leadership. More recently, we explored neural resonance and co-regulation — the ways nervous systems influence one another through presence, attunement, and shared safety.

Now we move one layer deeper into the neurobiology underlying those relational experiences.

Many thoughtful readers naturally begin wondering:

What is actually happening inside the brain and body when human connection becomes healing?

While no single mechanism explains the full complexity of relational experience, modern interpersonal neurobiology offers a growing understanding of how human nervous systems communicate safety to one another. Among the most discussed — and often misunderstood — aspects of this process are what researchers have termed mirror neuron systems.

Before exploring the science directly, however, let me begin with an observation from my own therapy office.

Sophie, my therapy dog, continues to fascinate me.

During in-office therapy sessions, she makes choices. Sometimes she settles quietly at my feet. Other times — without prompting — she rises and gently curls beside a client who is visibly distressed. She does not respond to the content of the conversation itself. She responds to something deeper and more physiological: shifts in breathing, posture, muscular tension, facial expression, tone, and emotional energy.

Again and again, clients describe similar experiences:

"I didn't realize how tense I was until she came over."

"My body softened when she sat beside me."

"Something about that moment helped me breathe again."

What Sophie is responding to — and what clients are experiencing — reflects a central principle of human neurobiology: Nervous systems are exquisitely sensitive to one another.

Healing does not occur through insight alone. It unfolds through moment-to-moment exchanges of safety between living systems.

When people imagine therapeutic change, they often picture insight: understanding patterns, naming emotions, making meaning of the past. All of those processes matter deeply. But alongside the words, something quieter and profoundly biological is also taking place.

When two people sit together in relative safety and attunement, measurable physiological shifts often occur. Research in interpersonal neurobiology and affective neuroscience has documented partial synchronization of breathing rhythms, changes in heart rate variability, shifts in facial musculature, modulation of limbic activation, and increasing ventral vagal engagement within safe relational interaction.

Clients frequently describe these shifts without scientific language.

One woman once told me, “You didn’t say anything extraordinary... but for the first time my body felt like it could rest.”

That experience is not accidental.

It reflects the nervous system's built-in capacity for relational state transmission.

Mirror neurons are often described in popular psychology as the brain's "imitation system" — neurons that activate both when we perform an action and when we observe another individual performing that same action. Originally identified through primate research, these systems appear to contribute to action understanding, empathy, emotional learning, and social responsiveness.

At times, however, mirror neurons have been oversimplified in popular discussions. They are not a complete explanation for human connection. Rather, they function as one component within a much larger relational neurobiology network that includes limbic resonance, autonomic signaling, right-hemisphere attunement, facial and vocal micro-cue detection, and the ventral vagal social engagement system described by Stephen Porges.

Taken together, these systems help explain how human beings continuously read and respond to one another beneath conscious awareness.

When we are in the presence of someone who feels grounded, emotionally available, and physiologically safe, our nervous system is constantly taking in subtle information: facial expression, vocal tone, breathing rhythm, posture, pacing, eye contact, and micro-movements. These cues inform what Porges calls neuroception — the nervous system's rapid, automatic assessment of safety or danger.

When enough cues of safety are detected, the body gradually reorganizes itself accordingly.

This is why calm can, quite literally, be borrowed.

Earlier in the book, we explored how infants depend on caregiver co-regulation to learn emotional settling. Developmental research consistently demonstrates that repeated experiences of being soothed in relationship gradually become internalized as self-regulation capacity.

The encouraging reality is that the nervous system retains this plasticity across the lifespan.

Trauma may obscure access to relational safety, but it rarely eliminates the underlying capacity entirely. When adults repeatedly experience safe, attuned connection, something important begins occurring within the nervous system.

What was once borrowed gradually becomes owned.

Clients often describe this transition in deeply personal ways: "At first I could only calm down when I was here."

"Now I'm starting to feel that steadiness show up at home."

"It feels like my body is learning a new normal."

From a neurobiological perspective, this reflects experience-dependent plasticity. The nervous system updates its predictions about safety through repeated lived experience.

Within the Relational Nervous System Integration Model™, this marks another important developmental movement. Earlier stages focused heavily on reducing overwhelm and restoring stabilization because survival physiology had become dominant. As integration deepens, however, the nervous system increasingly begins reorganizing around connection rather than protection alone.

Compassion, from this perspective, is not merely an emotional attitude or moral virtue. It is an embodied regulatory state.

When a person is genuinely grounded and attuned, certain physiological patterns tend emerging naturally. Facial muscles soften. Vocal tone becomes warm and prosodic. Eye contact becomes steady but nonintrusive. Breathing slows. Muscular tension decreases.

These signals communicate something profoundly important to the observing nervous system:

There is no immediate danger here.

This is one reason presence often matters more than perfect words.

As Daniel J. Siegel reminds us in his description of the mind as an "embodied and relational, emergent, self-organizing process," regulation is never purely internal. It is continuously shaped within the space between people.

Healing accelerates when the nervous system repeatedly experiences safety in connection.

At the same time, it is important to clarify what healing connection does not require.

It does not require perfect attunement.

Disconnection is inevitable in all human relationships. Tone is misread. Timing fails. Misunderstandings occur. What builds resilience is not perfection, but repair.

Returning after misunderstanding. Re-establishing connection. Naming rupture without blame. Softening defensiveness. Remaining emotionally present long enough to reconnect.

These moments teach the nervous system something profoundly corrective: relationship can remain safe even when imperfect.

Repeated repair gradually builds what attachment researchers describe as earned security — the growing confidence that closeness does not inevitably end in abandonment, chaos, humiliation, or danger.

This is especially important because trauma often leaves the nervous system carrying a deeply encoded expectation: Closeness equals danger.

For this reason, healing rarely unfolds through isolation alone. Solitude can certainly be restorative, and the ability to be comfortably alone is developmentally important. But sustained trauma recovery almost always requires some form of safe relational experience because the nervous system heals most fully through updated relational prediction.

One client summarized this shift beautifully:

"I used to think healing meant being strong enough not to need anyone. Now I think it means learning how to feel safe with the right people."

That insight represents a profound developmental turning point.

As you move through your own daily interactions, it may be helpful to begin noticing subtle shifts in your body before, during, and after emotionally significant conversations. What happens to your breathing? What happens to your shoulders, jaw, posture, or internal sense of spaciousness? Do certain relationships consistently leave your system more regulated while others reliably produce contraction or vigilance?

These observations are not judgments. They are relational data.

Over time, this awareness helps the nervous system differentiate more clearly between relationships that support regulation and relationships that consistently require protection.

And as this relational awareness deepens, another important layer of healing naturally begins emerging into focus.

Many individuals start recognizing that their longstanding attachment patterns — the ways they approach closeness, trust, vulnerability, distance, conflict, and protection — become increasingly visible within relationships.

This raises the next important question: How do early attachment patterns continue shaping adult relationships, and how can those patterns gradually be reorganized through the capacities we are now developing?

That is where we now turn. Because resonance opens the door.

Attachment often determines what happens once we walk through it.

Chapter 20 - Building Resilience

"Small shifts, repeated consistently, create large changes over time." —Bruce H. Lipton

In the previous chapter, we explored something deeply hopeful: the nervous system is not designed to regulate in isolation. Through co-regulation, neural resonance, and repeated experiences of safe connection, the body can gradually begin internalizing steadiness that was once available only through others.

At this point in the Relational Nervous System Integration Model™, however, another practical and deeply important question naturally begins emerging: What happens when you are alone?

What happens at two in the morning, during a difficult conversation, or on an ordinary Tuesday afternoon when your body begins bracing for danger that is not actually present?

Co-regulation opens an essential doorway into healing. But as integration deepens, the nervous system gradually begins learning something equally important: steadiness can increasingly be carried from within.

Not perfectly. Not continuously. And certainly not all at once.

But reliably enough that the body slowly begins trusting that regulation remains accessible even when no one else is in the room.

Within the developmental arc of the Relational Nervous System Integration Model™, this chapter marks another important movement from insight into embodiment. Earlier chapters focused on stabilization, attachment, identity integration, emotional regulation, co-regulation, and relational resonance. Now the emphasis shifts toward building sustainable patterns of nervous system care that can hold under the ordinary pressures of daily life.

Because regulation is rarely a single technique mastered once and permanently retained.

It is a rhythm. A practice.

A relationship with the nervous system that strengthens gradually through repetition, adjustment, flexibility, and an increasing amount of self-compassion.

Like any meaningful developmental process, it also comes with obstacles — not because you are doing it wrong, but because the nervous system is often learning patterns that initially feel unfamiliar.

Rachel's early experience with regulation illustrates this beautifully.

"At first," she told me, "trying to calm myself made everything worse. My mind raced, my body fidgeted, and within seconds I was frustrated that I couldn't do it properly."

Rachel did not lack discipline or motivation. Her nervous system had simply learned, through years of chronic stress, that stillness was not always associated with safety. For many trauma survivors, when the external world grows quiet, the internal world initially becomes louder. Vigilance does not automatically switch off simply because we consciously decide it should.

So rather than approaching regulation as a performance she needed to perfect, we shifted the frame entirely. The question became less about: "How do I force myself to calm down?" and more about

"How do I learn to work with my nervous system instead of against it?"

That reframing alone often reduces a surprising amount of internal pressure.

This distinction matters enormously within the Relational Nervous System Integration Model™. Healing is not built through harsh self-control. It develops through increasing collaboration between awareness, physiology, and compassionate self-leadership.

When a nervous system has spent years organized around heightened readiness, meaningful change rarely comes through occasional bursts of effort. What the body responds to most reliably is predictable, repeated experience.

In neurobiological terms, this reflects experience-dependent plasticity: small inputs delivered consistently over time gradually reshape autonomic expectations and neural pathways.

For this reason, brief and sustainable practices often produce far more durable change than intense efforts performed sporadically. Rather than thinking only in terms of isolated techniques, it becomes more useful to think in terms of building a regulation rhythm — a gentle structure that supports the nervous system throughout the ordinary movements of daily life.

Morning practices, for example, often carry disproportionate importance because the nervous system begins organizing its baseline tone early in the day. Many individuals living with chronic stress wake already carrying subtle mobilization: shallow breathing, muscular tension, anticipatory thinking, or a diffuse sense of urgency before the day has even begun.

A short parasympathetic-supportive practice can begin shifting that baseline gently.

This does not need to be elaborate. Sitting quietly for a few moments, placing one hand on the chest and another on the abdomen, and taking several slower diaphragmatic breaths may already begin communicating safety to the body. Some individuals find it helpful to inhale for a count of four and exhale for a count of six, allowing the longer exhalation to support parasympathetic settling.

Thoughts inevitably arise during these moments. The goal is not the elimination of thinking. The goal is the return.

Rachel initially became discouraged because her mind wandered constantly. But over time she realized that each nonjudgmental return to the breath was quietly strengthening regulation capacity itself. She began with one minute. Within several weeks, her body comfortably tolerated five — not because she forced it, but because the practice gradually stopped feeling threatening.

This illustrates another important principle: dosage matters.

For some nervous systems, three grounded breaths practiced consistently produce more integration than ten strained minutes performed under internal pressure.

Evening practices often serve a different function entirely. If morning helps establish baseline organization, evening teaches the nervous system that the day can safely end.

Many trauma survivors arrive at night physically exhausted but physiologically alert. Their bodies remain prepared for vigilance long after external demands have passed.

Practices such as Progressive Muscle Relaxation, originally developed by Edmund Jacobson, can be especially helpful here because they teach the body through contrast. By gently tensing and releasing different muscle groups, individuals begin recognizing the difference between bracing and softening.

This strengthens interoceptive awareness — the ability to sense and influence internal physiological state — which is often diminished in chronically stressed systems.

Importantly, regulation practices remain adaptive rather than rigid. If a particular exercise increases overwhelm, the intensity can be reduced. If sleep arrives quickly, that is useful information. If certain parts of the body carry pain or injury, they can simply be skipped.

The nervous system responds best to responsiveness, not force.

Midday regulation often serves yet another purpose: interrupting accumulated activation before it fully escalates.

Visualization practices, when understood correctly, are not forms of denial or forced positivity. They function as nervous system rehearsal through felt sensory experience. When individuals recall moments of safety with sufficient sensory detail — warmth, sound, texture, light, physical settling — overlapping neural networks activate in ways that partially resemble lived experience.

The body begins remembering that regulated states exist and remain accessible.

Rachel initially struggled with visualization.

"I can't picture anything," she said repeatedly.

So we shifted away from imagery entirely and focused first on sensation: the weight of her body in the chair, the feeling of air on her skin, the rhythm of her breathing.

For many nervous systems, sensation becomes the doorway through which imagery and emotional safety gradually emerge.

And again, the principle remained the same: small, tolerable doses.

Within the Relational Nervous System Integration Model™, this gradual pacing is not incidental. It reflects the nervous system's need for manageable experiences of safety that do not overwhelm existing protective structures.

What ultimately transformed Rachel's experience was not mastering one perfect technique. It was building a rhythm her nervous system slowly learned to trust.

Her pattern became intentionally simple: one minute of belly breathing before coffee each morning, a thirty-second reset in the car before work, and muscle relaxation at night while listening to familiar music.

At first, the practices felt almost too small to matter.

But what she was teaching her nervous system was profound: "I know how to come back."

About five weeks into the process, she experienced a difficult interaction with a family member that previously would have dysregulated her for hours. This time, she noticed the early physiological cues: tightening in her chest, shortened breathing, accelerating thoughts.

Instead of spiraling automatically, she paused, placed a hand on her abdomen, and took several slower breaths.

Later she reflected quietly: "I didn't feel perfect. But I didn't lose myself."

That sentence captures the essence of integration beautifully.

Within the Relational Nervous System Integration Model™, progress is not measured by the elimination of activation. It is measured increasingly by continuity of self during activation — the growing ability to remain connected to awareness, regulation, and internal leadership even while stress is present.

Over time, many individuals begin noticing subtle but deeply meaningful signs of integration. They recognize activation earlier. They intervene sooner. The jaw tightens and they notice. The shoulders rise and they notice. The breath shortens and they notice.

Instead of waiting until overwhelm fully erupts, they begin responding while activation remains manageable.

Regulation gradually shifts from emergency response into ongoing nervous system stewardship.

At the same time, it is important to remember what we explored in the previous chapter: human nervous systems continue regulating most efficiently within safe connection. Self-regulation and co-regulation are not opposing capacities. They strengthen one another.

Practicing breathing with a trusted friend, walking rhythmically beside someone safe, or simply sitting quietly near a calm nervous system often accelerates integration because human biology remains fundamentally relational.

The goal is not radical independence from others.

The goal is flexible access to both self-regulation and co-regulation.

Together, these capacities gradually form the foundation of earned security.

And as regulation rhythms become more stable, many people begin growing curious about something measurable. They begin wondering whether it is possible to actually observe the nervous system learning in real time.

That question leads naturally into the next stage of the journey.

Because as Part Three draws toward completion, we begin preparing for an important transition within the Relational Nervous System Integration Model™ — moving from foundational regulation and relational integration toward increasingly measurable coherence, resilience, and embodied transformation.

In the next chapter, which opens Part Four, we will explore heart rate variability (HRV) training — a research-supported window into nervous system flexibility and coherence that allows individuals to observe regulation patterns directly while strengthening the physiological foundations of resilience itself.

Sometimes one of the most encouraging experiences the body can have is simple, tangible evidence that change is already underway.

PART IV - Putting Trauma to Rest

Within the Relational Nervous System Integration Model™, the work of healing unfolds developmentally. Earlier stages focused on stabilization, regulation, embodiment, attachment, identity integration, and the gradual restoration of relational safety. As those capacities strengthen, the nervous system becomes increasingly able to remain present without becoming overwhelmed by activation.

This creates the conditions for a deeper phase of healing.

Traumatic memories often remain stored in fragmented networks of sensation, emotion, body state, and belief. When these networks are triggered, the nervous system may react as though the original experience is still occurring in the present moment. The body mobilizes. Emotions intensify. Protective patterns activate automatically, often outside conscious awareness.

Importantly, this does not mean the nervous system is malfunctioning.

It means unresolved experiences have not yet been fully integrated.

Part Four focuses on therapies and practices that work directly with these deeper memory systems. The approaches explored in this section — Heart Rate Variability training, Emotional Freedom Technique, EMDR, and the Flash Technique — each approach trauma from slightly different angles, but they share a common therapeutic aim: helping the brain and nervous system complete processing that was interrupted when the original experience exceeded the system's capacity to integrate it safely.

Within the Relational Nervous System Integration Model™, this stage represents a movement from foundational regulation into deeper memory integration and reconsolidation. The nervous system is no longer working solely to survive overwhelming activation. It is increasingly developing the capacity to revisit previously unresolved experiences while remaining connected to present-day safety, regulation, and internal leadership.

As traumatic memories become more integrated, something profoundly important begins happening.

The past gradually loses its physiological immediacy.

The nervous system becomes less organized around anticipation of old danger and more available for present-moment living, flexible connection, creativity, and meaningful engagement with life as it is now rather than as it once was.

This is not forgetting the past. It is no longer being governed by it.

Chapter 21 Training the Heart to Lead

"Feelings are not just in the mind. They are in the body as well." —Antonio Damasio

As Part Three drew to a close, we explored how regulation gradually becomes more than an emergency response. Through repeated experiences of self-regulation and co-regulation, the nervous system begins learning steadiness as an increasingly familiar state rather than a temporary interruption of stress.

This naturally brings us to an important next stage within the Relational Nervous System Integration Model™.

Once stabilization, embodiment, relational safety, and internal leadership have strengthened sufficiently, many individuals begin wondering whether regulation can become more measurable, trainable, and physiologically reliable in daily life. In other words, if the nervous system can learn survival patterns through repetition, can it also be trained toward greater coherence and resilience through repeated physiological practice?

Part Four begins answering that question directly.

Within the Relational Nervous System Integration Model™, this stage represents a movement from foundational regulation into increasingly measurable nervous system integration. Earlier chapters focused on building awareness, expanding the window of tolerance, strengthening co-regulation, and establishing sustainable rhythms of self-care. We now begin exploring approaches that work more directly with autonomic organization and memory integration itself.

Heart Rate Variability training offers one particularly compelling doorway into this process because it allows individuals to observe, influence, and strengthen nervous system flexibility in real time.

By the time many people reach this stage of healing, something important has already begun shifting internally. Regulation no longer feels like a matter of willpower or positive thinking alone.

Instead, there is a growing lived awareness that the body itself can learn safety — and that this learning unfolds through repeated physiological experience.

From that place, a deeper and very natural question often emerges: "If my nervous system can be trained... can I actually influence my emotional state in real time?"

When Sarah first voiced this in session, she did so with a tired half-laugh. "I wish I could change my emotions," she said. "That would be a superpower."

What she did not yet realize was that the capacity she was longing for was already present — not simply in her thoughts, but in the ongoing communication between her heart, her brain, and her autonomic nervous system.

For much of modern medical history, the brain was viewed as the unquestioned command center of emotional life. Feelings were assumed to originate primarily in cortical processing and travel downward into the body, where the heart merely responded passively to instructions.

Over the past several decades, however, neuroscience and psychophysiology have painted a far more reciprocal picture. The heart communicates continuously with the brain through multiple pathways, most prominently through the vagus nerve and related afferent systems. In fact, a substantial portion of neural traffic travels upward from the body to the brain rather than only downward from the brain into the body.

These ascending signals influence emotional regulation, attentional stability, cognitive flexibility, and the nervous system's ongoing assessment of safety or threat. From this perspective, emotional state is not produced by cognition alone. It is shaped moment by moment by the rhythm, timing, and organization of physiological signals moving throughout the system.

This is where Heart Rate Variability — or HRV — becomes especially relevant.

Many people initially assume that a healthy heart beats with perfect mechanical regularity, like a metronome. In reality, a well-regulated nervous system looks far more like a skilled jazz musician: flexible, adaptive, and responsive to changing conditions.

Heart Rate Variability refers to the subtle variation in timing between consecutive heartbeats. These fluctuations reflect the dynamic interplay between sympathetic mobilization and parasympathetic recovery.

In general, higher HRV is associated with greater autonomic flexibility, emotional resilience, and adaptive capacity. Lower HRV often reflects a system that has become more rigid, threat-focused, or chronically taxed by prolonged stress.

A growing body of research has linked higher HRV with improved emotional regulation, stronger executive functioning, greater stress resilience, and more efficient recovery following activation. Conversely, chronically reduced HRV is commonly observed in individuals experiencing prolonged stress exposure, anxiety disorders, burnout, and trauma-related dysregulation.

What makes HRV especially meaningful within trauma recovery is this: it is not fixed.

The nervous system can strengthen coherence and flexibility through repeated practice.

Within the Relational Nervous System Integration Model™, this idea is profoundly important. Healing is not viewed as merely intellectual insight or symptom suppression. It involves helping the nervous system repeatedly experience new physiological patterns until those patterns gradually become more familiar and accessible.

Under conditions of chronic stress, heart rhythms often become erratic and less synchronized. From the brain's perspective, incoming physiological signals appear noisy and inconsistent, which can contribute to emotional reactivity, narrowed attention, and reduced cognitive clarity.

When heart rhythms shift into a smoother and more ordered pattern — a state commonly referred to as physiological coherence — something different begins happening. The brain receives more stable afferent input associated with regulation and safety. Emotional processing becomes more efficient. Attentional stability improves. Many individuals describe a growing sense of internal organization and clarity.

Importantly, coherence is not mystical. It is measurable autonomic organization.

Sarah's first experience of coherence surprised her.

"I didn't feel numb," she said afterward. "And I didn't feel overwhelmed. I just felt... clear. Like my system finally stopped arguing with itself."

That description captures beautifully what many people report when the autonomic nervous system begins functioning with greater integration.

While HRV is influenced by many variables, two accessible practices consistently strengthen coherence when paired together.

The first is rhythmic breathing.

When breathing slows to approximately five or six breaths per minute through smooth and even inhalation and exhalation, vagal influence on the heart increases and heart rhythm patterns often begin organizing more coherently. This is not about forcing deep breaths or controlling the body rigidly. In fact, effortful breathing can sometimes increase activation.

What matters most is rhythm, smoothness, and consistency.

Many individuals find a gentle pattern helpful, such as inhaling for roughly five seconds and exhaling for five or six seconds. Over time, this rhythmic pacing begins supporting greater parasympathetic flexibility and autonomic balance.

The second element involves warm emotional engagement.

Research and clinical observation both suggest that coherence strengthens when rhythmic breathing becomes paired with a genuine embodied emotional state such as appreciation, gratitude, care, affection, or compassion.

It is important to clarify this carefully. The goal is not forced positivity or denial of difficult emotion. The nervous system responds most reliably to felt experience rather than intellectual effort alone.

For individuals with significant trauma histories, accessing positive emotional states may initially feel surprisingly difficult. This is not resistance or failure. It often reflects protective physiology. The nervous system has spent years prioritizing vigilance over openness.

In these moments, it often helps to begin very concretely: the memory of a dog resting quietly beside you, sunlight warming your skin, a peaceful place once visited, or the steady presence of someone who felt safe.

Small, believable experiences are more regulating than exaggerated emotional effort.

Together, rhythmic breathing and warm emotional engagement begin creating a reinforcing feedback loop. The heart sends increasingly coherent signals upward, and the brain correspondingly stabilizes emotional tone, attention, and autonomic organization.

Michael experienced this shift quite unexpectedly.

For years, he had lived with sudden surges of anxiety that seemed to emerge without warning. Traditional grounding strategies helped somewhat, but often only after prolonged effort. When we introduced HRV coherence training, he approached it skeptically.

Then one afternoon, while practicing slow rhythmic breathing and focusing on the quiet warmth he associated with his dog resting beside him, something shifted.

"It was like finding an internal reset button," he told me later. "My chest softened. My thoughts slowed. And for once, it didn't take an hour."

The practice did not erase his trauma history. What it offered instead was something equally important: a repeatable physiological pathway back toward regulation.

His nervous system now had a reference point it could return to.

Like many of the regulation practices explored earlier in this book, HRV training works best when approached gently and consistently. Most individuals benefit far more from short, repeatable practice than from intense effort performed inconsistently. A few minutes in the morning, brief resets during the day, and calming practice in the evening often create meaningful change over time.

With repetition, the nervous system gradually begins recognizing coherence as familiar territory.

People often notice subtle but meaningful changes first. They recover more quickly from stress. They recognize activation earlier. They think more clearly under pressure. Emotional swings feel less abrupt and consuming.

These are not personality changes. They are signs of physiological learning.

Several predictable obstacles commonly emerge early in HRV practice. Some individuals struggle accessing positive emotional states. Others find it difficult to sustain attention. Many worry they are "doing it wrong."

Importantly, these concerns are not signs of failure. They are often predictable echoes of survival physiology itself. The nervous system learns coherence through repetition and tolerable experience, not through perfect performance.

Sometimes external supports such as paced breathing applications or biofeedback devices provide useful scaffolding during this phase of learning. But ultimately, the deeper goal is not technological dependence.

It is increasing nervous system literacy.

As HRV practice becomes integrated, many individuals begin describing a subtle but profound change in their relationship with themselves.

Several months into her practice, Sarah reflected:

"I'm not just managing my emotions anymore. I can feel when something is off... and I know how to guide myself back."

That statement captures the deeper gift of coherence training beautifully. The goal is not rigid control over emotional experience.

It is growing collaboration between heart, brain, body, and awareness — the very integration that supports earned security over time.

Within the Relational Nervous System Integration Model™, this represents another important developmental movement. The nervous system is no longer functioning primarily as a reactive survival system. Increasingly, it becomes capable of organized self-regulation, flexible adaptation, and embodied recovery even under stress.

And as coherence becomes more familiar, another important question naturally begins emerging.

How do we carry this physiological steadiness into the complexity of real-world relationships, environments, and emotionally activating situations?

That is where we now turn next.

Because coherence practiced in isolation is only the beginning. The deeper work involves learning how to sustain regulation, flexibility, and connection inside the unpredictability of ordinary life itself.

Chapter 22 - From Regulation to Resilience

"Resilience is the ability to recover from stress and return to balance." — Stephen Porges

In the previous chapter, we explored Heart Rate Variability training and the growing capacity of the nervous system to move toward physiological coherence. We examined how the heart, brain, and autonomic nervous system communicate continuously with one another, and how repeated experiences of coherence gradually strengthen regulation, clarity, and emotional steadiness.

As these practices become more familiar, however, something subtle but deeply important begins shifting.

Regulation stops feeling like a technique that is used only during crisis. Instead, it gradually becomes a way of inhabiting experience.

Within the Relational Nervous System Integration Model™, this marks another important developmental movement. Earlier phases of healing focused primarily on survival: reducing overwhelm, expanding the window of tolerance, strengthening embodiment, developing internal leadership, and restoring relational safety. More recently, we explored how coherence can help stabilize autonomic functioning and increase nervous system flexibility.

Now the question becomes less: "How do I calm myself down?" and more "How do I remain internally organized while life continues unfolding around me?"

That shift represents the beginning of resilience.

Lisa's experience illustrates this transition beautifully. When she first began HRV coherence work, she approached it cautiously. Anxiety had accompanied much of her adult life, surfacing quickly and lingering long after stressful situations had passed.

Yet over time, something gradually reorganized inside her system.

"It's like having an internal compass now," she told me. "I still feel anxious sometimes — but I don't get lost inside it anymore."

That distinction is enormously important.

Resilience is not emotional numbness. It is not forced calm, rigid self-control, or the elimination of difficult emotion. Resilience reflects the growing capacity to remain connected to awareness, regulation, and self-leadership while emotional activation moves through the system.

Within the Relational Nervous System Integration Model™, this is one of the clearest markers that regulation is becoming integrated at the identity level rather than existing merely as an isolated skill.

The nervous system is beginning to trust itself.

Earlier in trauma recovery, many individuals experience emotion as destabilizing. Anxiety feels consuming. Conflict feels overwhelming. Shame feels absolute. Once activation begins, the nervous system may rapidly lose access to perspective, flexibility, or grounded awareness.

As coherence strengthens over time, however, many people begin noticing a quieter but profoundly meaningful shift: emotion and regulation can increasingly coexist.

Someone may feel anxiety while remaining capable of reflection. Anger may arise without immediately escalating into impulsive reaction. Vulnerability may become possible without collapse or withdrawal.

This does not happen because difficult emotions disappear.

It happens because the nervous system becomes more capable of holding emotional intensity inside a regulated physiological container.

That is resilience.

One of the most encouraging aspects of this phase of healing is that the changes are often observable in ordinary moments long before they feel dramatic internally. Individuals notice themselves recovering more quickly after conflict. They recognize activation earlier. They remain more present during emotionally charged conversations. Their thoughts retain greater clarity under pressure.

In many ways, the nervous system begins shifting from reactive functioning toward responsive functioning.

This difference becomes especially visible inside relationships.

Earlier in the healing journey, relational stress may have triggered rapid survival responses: shutting down, overexplaining, escalating defensively, withdrawing emotionally, people-pleasing, or becoming flooded with fear and shame. In those moments, the nervous system was not choosing freely. It was reacting from previously encoded survival pathways.

As resilience develops, however, increasing pause capacity begins emerging between activation and response.

A difficult conversation may still activate the body, but the individual remains more capable of noticing what is happening internally while it is happening. They may recognize tightening in the chest, acceleration in thought, or the impulse to withdraw — yet still retain enough organization to breathe, remain present, and respond more intentionally.

This is where coherence begins moving beyond isolated practice sessions and into lived relational experience.

And importantly, this shift often unfolds gradually rather than dramatically.

One client described realizing halfway through an argument with her spouse that she was no longer spiraling in the way she once had. "I could feel myself getting activated," she explained, "but I also felt another part of me staying grounded at the same time."

That dual awareness reflects increasing integration across the nervous system.

Earlier chapters explored the development of internal leadership and the strengthening of the observing self. Here, those capacities begin functioning under pressure rather than only during calm moments. Regulation is no longer something practiced exclusively in safe environments. It becomes increasingly accessible inside the complexity of ordinary life.

Within the Relational Nervous System Integration Model™, this represents an important developmental progression toward earned security.

Earned security does not emerge because life becomes perfectly predictable or emotionally easy. It develops because the nervous system gradually learns, through repeated experience, that activation does not inevitably lead to collapse, abandonment, chaos, or loss of self.

The body begins trusting its capacity to return.

This trust is deeply physiological.

Many trauma survivors unconsciously live with the expectation that strong emotional activation will overwhelm them permanently. As resilience develops, however, a different internal experience gradually emerges:

"I can feel this without losing myself."

"I can become activated and still come back."

"I can remain connected even when emotion rises."

These realizations often appear deceptively simple, but they represent profound nervous system reorganization.

One of the most important shifts at this stage of healing involves moving away from rigid avoidance of emotional discomfort. Earlier in recovery, individuals may understandably organize their lives around minimizing activation altogether. While stabilization remains essential, long-term healing eventually requires something more flexible.

The nervous system begins learning that emotional intensity itself is not necessarily dangerous. Grief can arise and settle. Conflict can occur and repair can follow. Anxiety can move through the body without fully taking over the system. Shame can surface without becoming identity.

This growing flexibility allows individuals to engage life more fully rather than structuring their entire existence around protection from discomfort.

And this is where resilience begins transforming identity itself.

People frequently describe subtle but meaningful changes in how they experience themselves:

"I trust myself more."

"I don't feel as fragile."

"I recover faster."

"I don't panic as quickly anymore."

"I can stay present longer."

These are not merely emotional improvements.

They are signs that the nervous system is reorganizing around increasing coherence, flexibility, and internal safety.

Importantly, resilience does not eliminate the need for co-regulation or supportive relationships. As we explored earlier, human nervous systems remain profoundly relational throughout life. What changes is that connection becomes less about desperate stabilization and more about mutual regulation, reciprocity, and authentic presence.

The individual no longer depends entirely on others to create emotional organization because increasing organization now exists internally as well.

This creates a very different relational experience.

Conflict becomes more navigable. Repair becomes more accessible. Emotional availability increases. Defensive posturing softens. Many people discover they can listen more fully because their nervous system is no longer working so intensely to protect itself during every emotionally charged interaction.

Over time, coherence begins influencing not only emotional regulation, but leadership, creativity, decision-making, and meaning-making more broadly. Energy previously consumed by vigilance and survival forecasting gradually becomes available for engagement with life itself.

This is one reason resilience often feels less like "coping" and more like freedom.

Not freedom from all pain or activation.

But freedom from being continuously governed by old survival patterns.

Within the Relational Nervous System Integration Model™, this stage serves another important function as well. As coherence and resilience deepen, the nervous system becomes increasingly capable of approaching unresolved emotional material without becoming overwhelmed by it.

This is a crucial developmental threshold.

Earlier in trauma recovery, deeper processing may have destabilized the system too quickly. But now, increasing physiological organization creates the conditions necessary for more direct trauma integration work.

In other words, regulation creates the conditions for resolution.

As resilience strengthens, many individuals notice that certain emotional charges still remain beneath the surface. Specific memories may continue carrying intensity. Certain triggers may still activate the body disproportionately despite increasing regulation skills.

This does not mean healing has stalled.

It often means the nervous system has become stable enough to begin approaching deeper unresolved material safely.

That is precisely where the next stage of healing begins.

Because once the nervous system can repeatedly find its way back toward regulation, it becomes increasingly possible to work directly with stored emotional memories without becoming consumed by them.

And that is where we now turn next.

In the coming chapter, we will explore Emotional Freedom Technique (EFT), a method that builds upon the regulatory foundation established here by helping the nervous system revisit and reorganize emotionally charged experiences in a way that is both embodied and accessible.

Where coherence helps stabilize the system, deeper trauma-processing approaches begin helping the nervous system release what it has been carrying for years.

The body is no longer learning only how to survive activation.

It is beginning to learn how to resolve it.

Chapter 23 - Emotional Freedom Technique

"Trauma is not just an event that took place sometime in the past; it is also the imprint left by that experience on mind, brain, and body." — Bessel van der Kolk

In the previous chapter, we explored the movement from regulation to resilience. We examined how coherence gradually becomes embodied through repeated experiences of physiological stability, emotional flexibility, and increasing internal leadership. Over time, the nervous system begins learning that activation does not inevitably lead to overwhelm, collapse, or loss of self.

As this foundation strengthens, an important developmental shift naturally begins emerging within the Relational Nervous System Integration Model™. The work is no longer focused only on helping the nervous system stabilize in the present. Increasingly, the system becomes capable of approaching unresolved emotional material that has remained physiologically active beneath the surface for years — sometimes decades.

At this stage, many individuals notice something paradoxical. Even as regulation improves, certain memories or emotional triggers may continue carrying disproportionate intensity. The body reacts quickly. Shame surges suddenly. Fear appears almost automatically. Particular situations continue activating emotional states that feel larger than the present moment alone would seem to justify.

This does not mean healing has failed. More often, it means the nervous system has finally become stable enough to begin processing material that previously would have been too overwhelming to approach safely.

That is where Emotional Freedom Technique — often referred to as EFT or "tapping" — can become especially valuable.

Within the Relational Nervous System Integration Model™, EFT represents another important movement in the integration process: helping emotionally charged material become reprocessed while the nervous system remains sufficiently regulated and connected to present-time safety. Unlike earlier stages of healing that focused primarily on stabilization and coherence, EFT begins working more directly with emotionally encoded memory networks themselves.

Monique's experience illustrates this transition beautifully.

When she first heard about EFT, she laughed — not dismissively, but with the weary skepticism of someone who had already tried many approaches that promised relief without fully reaching the body. After years of combat-related PTSD, chronic hypervigilance, and disrupted sleep, the idea that gently tapping on points along the face and upper body might influence her nervous system felt difficult to believe.

"And yet," she later reflected, "after that first session, something shifted. My body felt quieter. Not numb — just calmer. For the first time in years, I could breathe without bracing."

Her experience highlights something deeply important about trauma recovery: insight alone is often not enough.

Throughout this book, we have explored how trauma is not stored solely as narrative memory or conscious thought. While understanding the story matters deeply, unresolved trauma often remains encoded more powerfully within emotional memory networks, conditioned autonomic responses, body states, sensory associations, and procedural survival patterns.

This is one reason individuals may intellectually recognize that they are safe while their physiology continues responding as though danger remains present. The thinking brain understands. The body has not yet fully updated.

Within the Relational Nervous System Integration Model™, this distinction is critical. Healing requires more than cognitive insight. It involves helping the nervous system repeatedly experience safety while emotionally charged material is activated, allowing the body itself to learn that the danger belongs to the past rather than the present.

EFT works directly at this intersection between emotional activation and physiological regulation.

At its core, the process combines two experiences that rarely occur spontaneously together. First, the individual gently brings attention toward a specific emotional memory, body sensation, fear, image, or belief — enough to activate the associated neural network without overwhelming the system completely. Second, while remaining connected to that material, the person rhythmically taps on a sequence of acupressure points located primarily on the face and upper body.

From a nervous system perspective, this pairing appears to support a form of counterconditioning. The brain learns through association, and when previously distressing emotional material becomes repeatedly paired with simultaneous signals of safety, regulation, and parasympathetic engagement, the nervous system gradually begins updating its response.

The memory itself often remains intact. What changes is the intensity of the alarm attached to it.

Research into EFT continues evolving, but a growing body of studies suggests that tapping protocols may reduce activation within limbic structures such as the amygdala while simultaneously supporting parasympathetic regulation and reductions in stress hormone activity. Although the precise mechanisms are still being studied, the clinical pattern appears increasingly consistent: the nervous system becomes less reactive to previously overwhelming emotional material.

Importantly, EFT often feels different from more exposure-heavy approaches because the process is intentionally paced to remain relatively close to the window of tolerance we explored earlier. Rather than flooding the nervous system with overwhelming emotional intensity, EFT approaches traumatic material gradually while maintaining simultaneous regulation. This allows the nervous system to experience activation without becoming consumed by it.

Within the Relational Nervous System Integration Model™, this pacing is essential. The goal is not catharsis through overwhelm. The goal is integration through tolerable experience.

Amanda's story illustrates this beautifully.

She sought therapy after years of freezing whenever someone raised their voice. Intellectually, she understood where the reaction originated. Her childhood environment had been emotionally volatile and unpredictable, and her nervous system had learned early that raised voices often preceded danger. Even as an adult, however, her body reacted long before conscious reasoning could intervene.

When we introduced EFT, we moved slowly and carefully. Rather than beginning immediately with the most emotionally charged memories, we first focused on present-time physiological experience: the tightening in her chest, the urge to disappear, the shallow quality of her breathing.

As she tapped gently while staying connected to those sensations, something gradually shifted. Her shoulders softened. Her breathing deepened. The urgency in her nervous system began decreasing. Over time, she discovered — somewhat to her surprise — that she could remain emotionally present while recalling situations that previously would have pushed her immediately into shutdown.

Later she reflected: "Talking helped me understand. Tapping helped my body believe I was safe."

That distinction captures the role EFT often plays within trauma recovery remarkably well.

One of the most powerful aspects of EFT is that it frequently restores a felt sense of agency inside the nervous system itself. Many trauma survivors experience emotional activation as something that happens to them — sudden, involuntary, and difficult to interrupt once it begins. EFT offers a different experience. Rather than fighting the emotion or attempting to override it cognitively, the individual remains gently connected to the experience while simultaneously participating in regulation.

This creates a profoundly different internal relationship. The nervous system no longer experiences emotion as an uncontrollable force that inevitably overwhelms the self. Instead, the body gradually learns:

"I can remain connected to this feeling without losing myself."

Within the Relational Nervous System Integration Model™, this reflects another important developmental progression from reactive survival into embodied self-leadership.

Importantly, EFT tends to work most effectively when approached gradually and respectfully. Trauma processing rarely benefits from forcing the nervous system beyond its available capacity. More often, healing unfolds through manageable pieces: one sensation, one image, one emotional layer at a time. This titrated pacing allows the nervous system to metabolize emotional material without becoming retraumatized by the process itself.

As regulation capacity strengthens, many individuals notice meaningful shifts beginning to emerge naturally. Emotional recovery becomes faster. Triggers soften. Previously overwhelming memories lose some of their physiological immediacy. The body begins responding more flexibly to experiences that once activated automatic survival states.

EFT is also most effective when integrated with the broader regulatory foundation already established throughout this book. Coherence practices help stabilize the nervous system. Grounding and orienting strengthen present-time safety. Co-regulation supports emotional containment. EFT then helps release emotional charge that has remained physiologically unresolved inside the system.

Together, these approaches create a more complete rhythm of healing.

Within the Relational Nervous System Integration Model™, this integration is deeply intentional. Regulation creates enough safety for processing. Processing reduces the burden the nervous system has been carrying. As that burden decreases, increasing flexibility, connection, and resilience become possible.

It is also important to acknowledge honestly that many people initially feel skeptical about EFT. That skepticism is understandable. The practice can appear deceptively simple from the outside. But EFT does not depend primarily upon belief in order to be useful. What matters far more is the nervous system's response.

And the body tends to provide remarkably honest feedback. Relief — even partial or subtle relief — is meaningful information.

As Emotional Freedom Technique begins reducing stored emotional charge, many individuals notice that their nervous system gradually feels less burdened by constant defensive activation. Anxiety softens. Sleep often improves. Emotional reactivity becomes more manageable. The body begins carrying a growing sense of internal safety and flexibility.

And yet, even at this stage, some emotional material may continue holding residual intensity. Certain memories may remain partially unresolved. Some experiences may still feel physiologically “unfinished” despite meaningful progress in regulation and emotional flexibility.

This does not represent failure. More often, it signals that the nervous system is now sufficiently stable to move into even deeper forms of memory integration.

That transition brings us naturally into the next phase of healing.

While EFT excels at helping regulate the body while approaching distress, other trauma-processing approaches work even more directly with the brain’s memory networks themselves. Among the most well-researched of these approaches is Eye Movement Desensitization and Reprocessing — EMDR.

Where EFT helps the nervous system soften emotional charge while maintaining regulation, EMDR works more directly with the brain’s information-processing systems, helping unresolved experiences move toward adaptive integration.

And now, with greater resilience, stronger coherence, expanded capacity, and a more regulated nervous system in place, the system is often far better prepared for that deeper level of reprocessing work.

That is where we now turn next.

Chapter 24 - EMDR Therapy

"The past affects the present even without our being aware of it." — Francine Shapiro

In the previous chapter, we explored Emotional Freedom Technique and the growing capacity of the nervous system to approach emotionally charged material without becoming overwhelmed by it. We examined how regulation, coherence, grounding, and self-leadership create the physiological conditions necessary for deeper processing to occur safely.

Within the Relational Nervous System Integration Model™, this progression is deeply intentional.

Earlier stages of healing focused primarily on stabilization: helping the nervous system develop sufficient regulation, flexibility, embodiment, and relational safety to tolerate activation without immediately collapsing into survival physiology. More recently, we explored how approaches such as EFT help reduce emotional charge while maintaining present-time regulation.

Now we move into a deeper layer of integration work itself.

By the time many people arrive at EMDR, something important has already shifted inside their nervous system. Regulation is no longer purely theoretical. There is more space between trigger and response, more capacity to stay present, and more confidence that difficult internal experiences can be approached without immediate overwhelm.

And yet, certain memories may still linger.

They do not always appear as vivid cinematic flashbacks. More often, they surface indirectly: as sudden emotional drops, unexplained body tension, familiar waves of shame or fear, or reactions that feel disproportionately intense compared to the present moment. A tone of voice, a facial expression, a smell, or a subtle relational cue may activate a response that feels immediate and compelling even while the thinking mind recognizes that the current situation is objectively safe.

This is the clinical territory where Eye Movement Desensitization and Reprocessing — EMDR — often becomes especially helpful.

EMDR is not designed to force people to relive trauma, nor is its aim to erase memory. Rather, it works with the brain's inherent capacity to process and integrate experiences that were once too overwhelming to metabolize fully. When this process unfolds successfully, memories that once felt intrusive and physiologically immediate gradually begin settling into the past where they belong.

Throughout this book, we have returned repeatedly to one central organizing principle: the nervous system is designed to move experience toward integration unless it becomes overwhelmed.

Under ordinary conditions, experience tends to flow through a largely adaptive sequence. Sensory input is registered. Emotional meaning emerges. The prefrontal cortex helps contextualize what happened. The nervous system eventually returns toward baseline, and the experience becomes integrated into a coherent autobiographical narrative.

Trauma disrupts this natural flow.

When threat is too intense, too sudden, or too prolonged, the brain shifts into survival prioritization. Higher cortical integration gives way to defensive circuitry. Experience becomes stored in fragments — sensations, images, emotional charges, body states, and protective beliefs — rather than as a fully integrated memory.

This helps explain why traumatic memories often feel timeless. The body responds as though the danger is happening now, even when the rational mind knows otherwise.

Within the Relational Nervous System Integration Model™, this understanding is essential because it reframes trauma symptoms not as irrational dysfunction, but as incomplete integration. The nervous system continues reacting defensively because portions of the experience were never fully metabolized and contextualized.

EMDR helps the brain re-engage the processing that was interrupted.

One of the defining features of EMDR is bilateral stimulation — most commonly guided eye movements, though tapping or alternating tones may also be used. While the precise mechanisms continue to be studied, several well-supported models help explain why this process can be effective.

From an interpersonal neurobiology perspective, bilateral stimulation appears to support communication between hemispheric networks while maintaining what clinicians often call dual awareness: one part of attention anchored safely in the present while another gently approaches the past.

From a neurocognitive standpoint, EMDR also appears to engage the brain's limited-capacity working memory system in a therapeutically useful way. This explanation often helps analytically minded individuals understand the process more concretely.

Working memory functions as the brain's active mental workspace. It allows us to hold images, sensations, thoughts, and emotions online simultaneously. But working memory is inherently limited in capacity.

Traumatic memories tend to occupy this workspace with unusual intensity. When activated, they often arrive not as distant recollections, but as vivid sensory and emotional experiences accompanied by strong physiological charge.

During EMDR, the individual briefly activates aspects of the memory while simultaneously engaging in bilateral stimulation that also requires working-memory resources. Because working memory is finite, the brain cannot maintain the traumatic imagery at full emotional intensity while also performing the dual-attention task.

Over repeated sets, many clients notice predictable shifts. The image becomes less sharp. Emotional intensity decreases. The body softens. The memory begins feeling farther away and less immediate.

This is not suppression or avoidance.

It reflects a neurocognitive recalibration that allows the memory to become more flexible, integrated, and available for adaptive updating. Research on dual-attention tasks increasingly supports this mechanism, showing reliable reductions in emotional vividness and physiological intensity when working memory is taxed during recall of distressing sensory memories.

As the emotional charge softens, the brain becomes increasingly capable of integrating present-day information — adult perspective, contextual understanding, updated beliefs about the self, and awareness that the danger is no longer occurring.

Gradually, the nervous system learns something profoundly important: the event is over. The memory remains. But it no longer dominates the present.

One of the most persistent myths about EMDR is that it requires graphic retelling or prolonged emotional exposure. In well-conducted EMDR therapy, the opposite is often true.

The process begins with careful preparation. Clients develop grounding skills, orienting capacity, emotional regulation resources, and sufficient stabilization before trauma processing begins. Within the Relational Nervous System Integration Model™, this preparation phase is foundational rather than optional. It is what allows deeper processing to occur safely within the individual's expanding window of tolerance.

When processing begins, the client typically brings only a small piece of the memory into awareness — perhaps an image, body sensation, emotional feeling, or negative belief — while bilateral stimulation is applied. The emphasis is not on detailed storytelling. The focus remains on observing the nervous system's unfolding response while staying sufficiently connected to present-time safety.

Many clients describe the experience as surprisingly organic: "It felt like my brain was making connections on its own." Or "Images kept shifting without me trying to force anything." Or "My body just... settled."

The therapist's role is not to direct the content rigidly, but to support pacing, containment, orientation, and safety while the brain's natural integrative processes gradually come back online.

Mark, a forty-two-year-old paramedic, sought therapy after years of unexplained panic reactions. Certain sounds — sirens, alarms, even the sharp beep of a microwave — triggered sudden surges of activation. He could not identify one defining trauma memory, only a persistent sense that his body was overreacting automatically.

During EMDR, however, a fragment gradually surfaced: the sound of a cardiac monitor flatlining during his first year on the job. At the time, he had pushed past the moment and continued working without fully processing the shock.

As bilateral stimulation continued across sessions, Mark noticed subtle but meaningful changes. The sound in memory lost some of its sharp edge. His chest softened. A new cognition emerged spontaneously:

"I did everything I could."

In the weeks that followed, his real-world panic responses diminished significantly. The sound remained recognizable, but it no longer hijacked his nervous system automatically. The memory had finally become integrated into a broader and more coherent life narrative.

This points toward one of the most important distinctions within trauma recovery.

Unlike strategies that primarily manage symptoms, EMDR works more directly with the underlying memory networks continuing to drive present-day reactivity. When processing unfolds successfully, the nervous system no longer needs to maintain the same defensive mobilization around those cues.

A substantial research base now supports EMDR's effectiveness, particularly for PTSD and trauma-related conditions, with growing evidence for its usefulness across grief, attachment injury, medical trauma, and performance-related distress.

From a nervous system perspective, this makes profound sense. Once the brain fully metabolizes an experience, the body is freed from maintaining chronic defensive readiness around it. Energy previously bound in vigilance and protection becomes increasingly available for connection, creativity, flexibility, and engagement with life in the present.

At the same time, it is important to emphasize that EMDR works best when built upon adequate nervous system stability. For some individuals, this foundation develops relatively quickly. For others — particularly those with complex developmental trauma — more time in regulation, coherence, attachment repair, and somatic safety work may be essential before deeper reprocessing feels tolerable.

There is no universal timeline.

Healing respects readiness.

Within the *Relational Nervous System Integration Model™*, this pacing remains deeply important. Trauma processing is not about forcing the nervous system into activation before sufficient capacity exists to metabolize the experience safely. Integration unfolds most effectively when stabilization and processing remain appropriately balanced.

It is also important to recognize that EMDR is not the only pathway toward integration. Some nervous systems initially benefit from gentler approaches that reduce distress without requiring sustained direct attention on highly activating material. This is especially true when trauma feels highly overwhelming, preverbal, or easily destabilizing.

And this brings us naturally to the next stage of the journey.

As powerful as EMDR can be, there are moments when even carefully titrated memory work feels like more than the nervous system is ready to hold directly. For those situations, clinicians have developed innovative approaches that allow trauma activation to soften without requiring sustained conscious focus on the distressing material itself.

Among the most promising of these approaches is the Flash Technique — a low-distress method designed to help the brain loosen trauma's grip while the person's primary attention remains anchored in something neutral, positive, or emotionally regulating.

Within the Relational Nervous System Integration Model™, this represents another evolution in trauma integration work: helping the nervous system process unresolved material while minimizing unnecessary overwhelm and preserving regulation throughout the process.

Sometimes healing unfolds through direct engagement.

And sometimes the nervous system heals more efficiently when given permission to work just outside the spotlight of conscious attention.

That is where we now turn next.

Chapter 25 - The Flash Technique

"The mind naturally moves toward healing when it is not overwhelmed." — Philip Mansfield

In the previous chapter, we explored EMDR and the brain's remarkable capacity to resume processing experiences that were once too overwhelming to integrate fully. We examined how unresolved trauma often remains stored in fragmented emotional, sensory, and physiological networks, and how bilateral stimulation can help those memories gradually lose their immediacy and emotional intensity.

Within the Relational Nervous System Integration Model™, EMDR represented an important progression from foundational regulation into deeper memory integration. Earlier stages of healing focused on stabilization, embodiment, coherence, attachment repair, and emotional flexibility. More recently, we explored how approaches such as EFT and EMDR help the nervous system revisit unresolved material while remaining sufficiently connected to present-day safety.

And yet, clinicians working closely with trauma survivors eventually began noticing something important.

For some nervous systems — particularly those shaped by complex trauma, chronic overwhelm, dissociation, or very narrow windows of tolerance — even carefully titrated trauma processing could still feel like too much, too fast. Direct engagement with traumatic material sometimes activated the system more intensely than it could comfortably metabolize.

Out of this clinical reality, a quieter innovation emerged.

The Flash Technique, developed by Philip Mansfield, grew from a deceptively simple but profound observation: the brain appears capable of updating traumatic memory networks even when conscious attention remains directed elsewhere.

In other words, full emotional immersion is not always required for meaningful neural change to occur.

For many trauma survivors, this realization feels profoundly relieving.

Throughout much of the history of trauma treatment, a central assumption shaped clinical practice: in order to heal painful memories, individuals needed to face them directly and remain emotionally engaged until the distress subsided. For many people, this approach has indeed been deeply helpful and effective.

But trauma science has increasingly revealed something more nuanced about how the nervous system heals.

Sometimes the brain updates most efficiently not through overwhelming immersion, but through carefully regulated access to emotionally charged material while safety remains intact.

Within the Relational Nervous System Integration Model™, this represents another important refinement in our understanding of integration. Healing is not measured by how intensely a person can endure emotional activation. More often, durable integration occurs when the nervous system remains sufficiently regulated to process experience without becoming consumed by survival physiology.

The Flash Technique reflects this principle beautifully.

At first glance, Flash can seem almost counterintuitive. Unlike traditional exposure-oriented models, Flash does not ask clients to focus deeply on traumatic material. Instead, the nervous system remains anchored primarily in something neutral, pleasant, or emotionally regulating while the brain appears to carry out much of the processing outside focal awareness.

The traumatic memory is acknowledged, but only lightly and briefly. It is not explored in detail. It is not narrated extensively. It is not intentionally amplified. And yet, in well-conducted Flash work, many clients report meaningful shifts: memories feel more distant, emotional intensity decreases, physiological activation softens, and triggers gradually lose their immediacy.

The memory remains accessible. But the charge begins loosening.

To understand why this matters, it helps to look more closely at how emotional memory networks update within the brain and nervous system.

As we explored in the previous chapter, traumatic memories often become "sticky" because they remain strongly paired with autonomic activation. When a trauma network fully dominates attention, the nervous system recruits threat circuitry — particularly within the amygdala and related limbic structures — and shifts rapidly toward defensive mobilization or shutdown.

Flash works differently.

Rather than fully activating the trauma network, the technique appears to work upstream of intense autonomic escalation. The brain's primary attentional systems remain oriented toward safety, regulation, and present-time stability while the distressing material is activated only peripherally — sometimes merely as a brief mental label or distant awareness.

From the perspective of memory reconsolidation research, this distinction may be extremely important.

A growing body of neuroscience research suggests that emotional memories do not necessarily require maximal activation in order to update. Instead, they appear to require sufficient access to the network while new regulatory information is simultaneously present. Flash appears to capitalize on this window by allowing the traumatic memory to come online just enough for updating to occur without triggering full defensive mobilization.

Over repeated "flash" moments, many individuals experience what can best be described as a quiet decoupling:

the memory is still there, but the nervous system no longer treats it as an immediate threat.

Within the Relational Nervous System Integration Model™, this process represents another important form of nervous system learning. The body gradually discovers that traumatic material can exist within awareness without automatically requiring survival activation.

This can be especially meaningful for highly sensitive or easily overwhelmed nervous systems.

Clinically, Flash is often considered particularly useful when individuals dissociate rapidly during trauma work, experience strong somatic flooding, carry significant developmental trauma, feel intense anticipatory fear about trauma processing, or require preparatory work before more direct approaches such as EMDR feel tolerable.

In these situations, Flash often functions as a regulation-preserving bridge. It gently softens emotional intensity around traumatic material so that deeper processing — if needed later — becomes increasingly accessible.

Importantly, this is not avoidance. It is strategic titration.

The nervous system is being given something it profoundly needs: access without overwhelm.

One client described the experience this way: "I always thought trauma work meant bracing myself. With Flash, I didn't brace. I stayed connected to something pleasant, and somehow the memory just... loosened."

That sense of surprise is clinically meaningful.

Many trauma survivors unconsciously associate healing with endurance, emotional intensity, or sheer force of effort. Flash introduces a different nervous system lesson: safety and processing can coexist.

And sometimes, when the nervous system feels sufficiently safe, it updates more efficiently than when it is pushed into high activation.

At this point in the book, you may notice a coherent pattern gradually emerging across the methods we have explored. Although EFT, EMDR, HRV coherence training, and Flash differ significantly in technique, they share several foundational neurobiological principles.

The nervous system processes most effectively within tolerable activation.

Memory networks update best in the presence of regulation and safety.

Healing does not require overwhelming catharsis.

And integration occurs through repeated experiences in which previously threatening material becomes paired with increasing physiological organization and present-time safety.

What differs among these approaches is not the overall goal, but the doorway through which the nervous system approaches integration.

EMDR uses dual attention and working-memory competition to reduce emotional vividness and facilitate reprocessing. EFT combines mild activation with somatic calming and cognitive acceptance. Flash keeps primary attention anchored in safety while allowing peripheral memory activation and reconsolidation to occur.

Within the Relational Nervous System Integration Model™, these methods are best understood not as competing schools of thought, but as flexible pathways that can be matched to the nervous system's current readiness and needs.

Skilled trauma work often involves discerning which doorway the nervous system is most prepared to walk through at a particular moment.

One of the most important contributions of the Flash Technique is philosophical as much as clinical. It challenges the long-standing assumption that healing must necessarily be emotionally intense in order to be meaningful.

Instead, Flash reflects a growing recognition within trauma science: the nervous system often heals most efficiently when it feels safe enough to do so.

This does not mean all trauma can or should be resolved indirectly. Some memories benefit from more direct engagement once sufficient stabilization and resilience have been established. But for many individuals — especially those early in trauma recovery or highly sensitive to overwhelm — Flash offers something profoundly regulating: a way to begin without bracing.

Within the Relational Nervous System Integration Model™, this marks another important developmental progression. Earlier stages emphasized survival, stabilization, and regulation. More recent chapters have explored how the nervous system gradually becomes capable of deeper integration without losing contact with safety, embodiment, and internal leadership.

Now we begin seeing what happens when the emotional burden carried by the nervous system starts genuinely softening.

As emotional charge decreases through approaches such as Flash, EFT, and EMDR, many individuals notice subtle but deeply meaningful shifts. Their nervous system becomes more organized, more flexible, and less chronically defensive. Relationships often feel safer. Emotional recovery becomes faster. The body carries less anticipatory tension.

And yet, sustainable healing ultimately involves more than symptom reduction or isolated processing techniques.

The deeper goal of trauma recovery is learning how to live from this increasingly regulated and integrated state — in relationships, under stress, and throughout the ordinary complexity of daily life.

That is where we now begin widening the lens once again.

Because as deeper processing unfolds successfully, the nervous system gradually becomes less organized around protection and increasingly available for connection, meaning, creativity, and embodied presence.

In the next chapter, we will explore how these nervous-system shifts begin reshaping identity, relationships, emotional freedom, and long-term resilience itself.

The deepest goal of healing is not simply reducing symptoms.

It is the gradual return of flexible, embodied aliveness.

Epilogue - Continuing the Work

> *"The privilege of a lifetime is to become who you truly are."* — Carl Gustav Jung

As we concluded the previous chapter, we explored a hopeful and increasingly important realization emerging from modern trauma science: the nervous system often heals most effectively when it feels sufficiently safe to do so. Through approaches such as EFT, EMDR, and the Flash Technique, we examined how emotionally charged memories can gradually lose their physiological immediacy, allowing the body to release patterns of protection that were once necessary for survival.

Within the Relational Nervous System Integration Model™, these final chapters represented the movement from foundational regulation into deeper integration and reconsolidation. Earlier stages focused on stabilization, attachment, embodiment, emotional flexibility, co-regulation, and resilience. Over time, the nervous system gradually developed enough capacity to revisit unresolved material without becoming overwhelmed by it.

And now, as we arrive at the end of this journey together, an important truth becomes increasingly clear: the deepest goal of healing is not simply symptom reduction.

It is the gradual restoration of flexible, embodied aliveness.

If you have made it this far, you have already done something meaningful. You have not simply gathered information; you have begun learning to view your own experience through a different and, I hope, more compassionate lens. Along the way, we have explored how trauma lives within the nervous system, how it shapes perception and reaction, and why so many responses that once felt confusing or self-critical actually make profound biological sense when understood through the lens of adaptation and survival.

For many readers, that shift alone brings a quiet kind of relief. Not because everything suddenly changes overnight, but because the story begins softening around the edges. Shame loosens slightly.

Curiosity increases. The nervous system no longer appears as an enemy to defeat, but as an intelligent system that learned to protect as best it could with the information and experiences available at the time.

Throughout this book, one central theme has appeared again and again: insight matters, but the nervous system changes primarily through experience.

Trauma is rarely resolved through willpower, intellectual understanding, or positive thinking alone. Healing unfolds through safe, repeated, embodied moments in which the body gradually learns something new — that activation can rise and fall without catastrophe, that connection can become steady, that emotion can move through the system without destroying it, and that the present moment is no longer identical to the past.

Within the Relational Nervous System Integration Model™, this is the heart of integration itself. The nervous system gradually reorganizes through repeated experiences of regulation, safety, embodiment, coherence, relational attunement, and adaptive memory updating. Over time, what was once effortful begins becoming increasingly familiar.

This kind of learning takes time. It takes gentleness. And perhaps most importantly, it requires respect for the pacing of your nervous system.

If there is one message I hope you carry forward from these pages, it is this: nothing about your healing process is a personal failure.

Nervous system healing unfolds as a biological process at the speed of safety.

As regulation strengthens, the earliest signs of change are often subtle enough to miss if you are not looking carefully for them. You may notice that you recover slightly faster after stress. You may catch yourself sooner before spiraling into overwhelm. You may pause where you once reacted automatically. You may feel brief moments of steadiness that previously seemed impossible to access.

These shifts matter far more than they initially appear.

They are signs that the nervous system is beginning to trust new pathways.

Over time — through repetition, support, and continued practice — these small moments accumulate. What once required significant effort gradually begins feeling more natural. What once felt fragile becomes more reliable. The nervous system slowly develops increasing confidence in its own ability to return from activation, remain connected under stress, and move flexibly through experience without collapsing into old defensive patterns.

Within the Relational Nervous System Integration Model™, this is what earned internal security begins to look like physiologically. The body no longer organizes itself primarily around survival anticipation. Increasingly, it organizes around flexibility, recovery, connection, and presence.

It is also important to remember that trauma recovery is rarely linear.

There are seasons of clarity and seasons of fog. Periods of expansion and periods of contraction. At times the work may feel surprisingly accessible; at other moments, old tenderness may resurface in ways that feel discouraging or confusing.

From a nervous system perspective, however, this does not necessarily mean you are moving backward.

Healing often unfolds more like widening spirals than straight lines. As regulation and capacity increase, deeper layers sometimes become accessible for integration. What once could not safely emerge may now be ready for processing precisely because the nervous system has become stronger, more flexible, and more resilient than before.

Progress is not measured by the total absence of activation.

It is reflected in increased flexibility, quicker recovery, deeper self-awareness, and a growing continuity of self in the presence of stress.

Because nervous system change is experience-dependent, the practices explored throughout this book tend to work best when approached gently and consistently rather than rigidly or all at once. Most individuals benefit from choosing a small number of supportive practices and allowing them to become familiar companions over time: rhythmic breathing, orienting, grounding, coherence work, mindful embodiment, safe relational connection, or moments of intentional slowing throughout the day.

These experiences may appear deceptively simple.

But repeated consistently, they gradually weave together into a more stable internal environment — one capable of holding more of life without tipping so quickly into overwhelm or shutdown.

You are not trying to eliminate stress from your life.

You are gradually expanding your capacity to move through it while remaining connected to yourself.

For some readers, education and self-directed practice will support meaningful progress. Others may discover that their nervous system benefits from additional relational support along the way. If activation remains persistently overwhelming, if dissociation is frequent, or if certain memories continue carrying strong physiological intensity, working with a trauma-informed clinician can provide important containment, pacing, and co-regulation.

Within the Relational Nervous System Integration Model™, this too reflects nervous system wisdom rather than weakness.

Human beings heal most fully in relationship.

There is no hierarchy here. Needing support is not evidence of inadequacy. Very often, it simply means your nervous system learned, at some point in its history, that it had to carry too much alone.

Many readers appreciate having structured ways to continue integrating what they have learned. For those who find it helpful, additional reflections and exercises are available in the companion workbook associated with this material. Some people prefer independent exploration, others benefit from therapeutic guidance, and many move fluidly between the two over time.

The most important principle is not the exact format you choose. It is the spirit in which the work continues: slowly, respectfully, and in collaboration with your nervous system rather than in opposition to it.

If trauma has been part of your story, there may have been long seasons when your body felt confusing, unpredictable, or even at odds with your conscious intentions. I hope this journey has helped you recognize something more clearly.

Your nervous system has never been your enemy.

It has been an intelligent adaptive system doing its best to protect you with the information it had available at the time.

And one of the most hopeful truths we have explored together is this: what the nervous system learned, it can gradually relearn.

With enough safety, repetition, regulation, and compassionate attention, the system begins reorganizing itself. It softens. It becomes more flexible, more responsive, and more capable of remaining present within the life unfolding now rather than remaining governed primarily by the past.

Within the Relational Nervous System Integration Model™, this is ultimately the deeper aim of healing:

not perfection, not permanent calm, and not the elimination of all emotional pain, but increasing freedom to live with coherence, flexibility, connection, embodiment, and authenticity.

Wherever you find yourself as you close these pages, I want to leave you with one final encouragement.

You do not have to rush your healing.

You do not have to force your nervous system to change.

And you do not have to walk this path perfectly for it to work.

Steady, respectful steps — taken at the pace of safety — are more than enough.

In time, many people discover something quietly remarkable:

what once felt like survival gradually begins, little by little, to feel like living.

Contact and Follow Dr. Don Russell

Youtube: @russellhealinginstituteltd

Instagram: www.instagram.com/drdonrussell/
And www.instagram.com/dr.donrussell

Website: www.drdonrussell.com

And please leave an honest review back on Amazon. I am am grateful.

www.ingramcontent.com/pod-product-compliance
Lightning Source LLC
LaVergne TN
LVHW052245200926
848481LV00002B/282
* 9 7 9 8 9 9 4 0 7 5 6 0 9 *